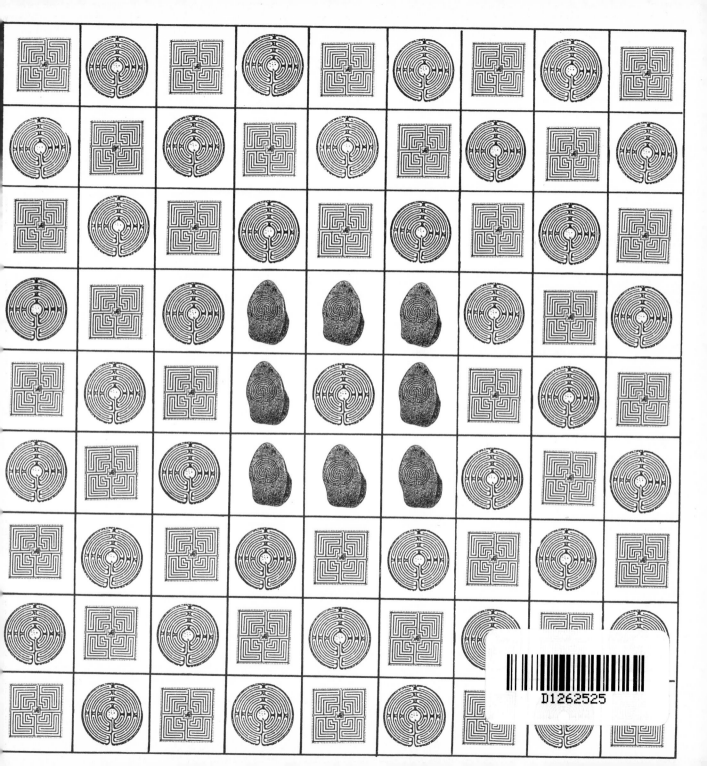

LABYRINTHS
ANCIENT MYTHS & MODERN USES

SIG LONEGREN

GOTHIC IMAGE
PUBLICATIONS

Copyright © Sig Lonegren 1991

First published in 1991 by
GOTHIC IMAGE PUBLICATIONS
7, High Street, Glastonbury, Somerset BA6 9DP

British Library Cataloguing in Publication Data
Lonegren, Sig 1941-
   Labyrinths: ancient myths and modern uses
   1. Myths
   I. Title
   306.4
   ISBN 0-906362-16-4

A CIP catalog record of this book is available
from the US Library of Congress.

Cover illustration and endpapers by Peter Woodcock
Illustrations by Jeff Saward/Caerdroia
and photographs by Sig Lonegren *except where indicated*

Designed and produced by Richard Elen
and set in Monotype Gill Sans at
Creative Technology Associates, Somerton, Somerset
Imagesetting by LP&TS, Aller, Somerset
Printed by Castle Cary Press, Somerset

ACKNOWLEDGEMENTS

I would like to thank the following people for the little hints, great ideas, and for the help they have given me in the creation of this book—Michael Bloom, Barbara Davies, Jamie George, David W. Gow, Phillip Hesselton, Kelley Hunter, Lucas and Jordan Lonegren, Lynn Lovell, Henry MacLean, Eleanor Ott, David Patten, and Wata. I would especially like to thank Mark Breen for his help with the movements of the planet Mercury and its relationship with the labyrinth; Donal Buchanan for his epigraphical information on the labrys, and especially his Celtic/Portugal/"Con"/labrys connection; my partner, Linda Cameron, for her proofreading and all her support; my editor at Gothic Image, Frances Howard-Gordon, for all her help and encouragement and understanding; Ronald Hutton, for his friendship and for his on-going correspondence and assistance with issues around pre-history; Twylah Nitsch for her encouragement to include some of the medicine wheel teachings; my sister Sally Lonegren for her help with the Jungian interpretation of dreams and myths; and Jeff Saward for reading an early draft of this book, and for all his marvellous illustrations.

I would also like to thank the following authors for their permission to use materials from their books or other publications:

Donal B. Buchanan for permission to use his epigraphic material concerning the Goidelic Celts' use of "con" in the Iberian peninsula.

Marija Gimbutas for her meander designs (seen here as Figure 29) of mesolithic figures from *The Language of the Goddess* ©1989 by Marija Gimbutas. Reprinted by permission of HarperCollins Publishers.

For the use of the illustration of the path of Mercury, (here Figure 53), from Joachim Schultz's *Movement and Rhythms of the Stars: A Guide to Naked-eye Observation of Sun, Moon, and Planets*, by kind permission of Floris Books, Edinburgh, Scotland.

My friend, Palden Jenkins, for permission to use a quote from page 86 of his *Living In Time*. (Bath, England: Gateway Books).

John Kraft for his inspiration and encouragement, and for his permission to use the illustration of the Köpmanholm double-pathed labyrinth and the paragraph with its story (pages 64-5), from his book *The Goddess In the Labyrinth* (Åbo Akademi, Sweden: Religionsvetenskaplinga Skrifter Nr 11). Also, for illustrations he sent me of Tibble, Lindbacke (drawn by Ivar Schnell), and Galgberget (drawn by S. Graulund) Labyrinths.

John Michell for permission to use the Planetary Magic Squares from page 124 of his *New View Over Atlantis* (London: Thames & Hudson).

Neil Michelsen (who passed away in May of 1990) and ASC for permission to use information on Mercury from his tables in *The American Ephemeris for the 20th Century (Noon/Midnight)* by Neil Michelsen, ASC Publications, San Diego, California.

My Seneca Grandmother, Twylah Nitsch, for permission to use The Pathways of Truth.

Labyrinth illustrations and relevant text from *Book of the Hopi*, by Frank Waters. Copyright ©1963 Frank Waters. Reprinted by permission of Viking Penguin, a division of Penguin Books Inc.

I am pleased by the synchronicity that *Labyrinths: Ancient Myths & Modern Uses* is being published by Gothic Image in 1991, the Year of the Maze in Great Britain. There will be talks, workshops, symposiums and gatherings discussing labyrinths. Old turf mazes will be maintained and restored. Mazes and labyrinths all over Britain are being honored. Perhaps this ancient sacred tool's time has indeed come 'round at last.

PUBLISHER'S NOTE

Some readers may find the combination of American English and 'English English' spellings used in this book unusual. Sig Lonegren is an American author, and as a result he uses American idioms and constructions in his writing. By keeping these, along with American spellings—which will be familiar to the majority of readers on both sides of the Atlantic—we feel that the essential 'Americanness' of Sig's writing is preserved for an international English readership. However, in cases where the American spelling or usage would be confusing to the reader, we have used the standard 'English English' spelling to ensure that the meaning is plain. We hope that readers will find this (somewhat unusual) scheme contributes to their enjoyment of this book, rather than detracting from it.

CONTENTS

ILLUSTRATIONS

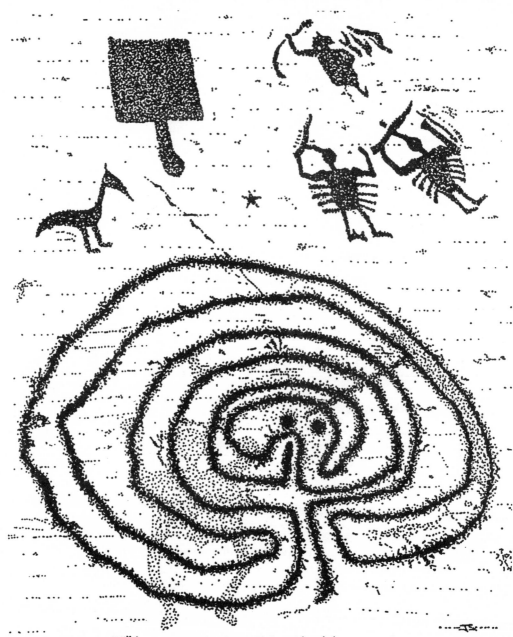

JEFF SAWARD/CAERDROIA

Labyrinth and Crane Dance—Val Camonica, Northern Italy

FOREWORD

THE STORY OF MAZES and labyrinths is as long and tortuous as their plans suggest. Mention mazes and most people think of Hampton Court or some other famous hedge maze. Mention labyrinths and some people recall the legend of Theseus and the Minotaur. Fewer still will know the labyrinth symbol which occurs around the world in different cultures, at different points in time, in places as diverse as Peru, Arizona, Iceland, Crete, Egypt, India and Sumatra. This symbol and its family of derivatives has been traced back over 3500 years; its origins are still mysterious.

At each of these incidents in time, the labyrinth symbol and the mythology that surrounds it have surfaced in a culture that has incorporated them into their lives for various purposes. Sometimes these episodes in labyrinth-time were short-lived, other times they flourished for hundreds of years and spread the concept far and wide. The media employed for its use have been many and varied: a simple symbol in a mythology, carved on a rockface, woven into the design on a basket, laid out on the ground with water-worn stones on shorelines, in coloured stone or tiles on the floors of churches and cathedrals or cut into the living turf—to name a few. Often the stories told of the labyrinth have been adapted for local use. Sometimes the design is altered or developed, but more often the symbol of the labyrinth is employed with no significant variation. The lines of contact between these widely-spaced bursts of labyrinth consciousness are difficult to trace; much remains to be discovered, but each represents one turn on the tortuous pathway of the labyrinth as it has danced its way around the world. Each of these episodes has left behind a scatter of examples that have survived to this day; scattered words from the story of the labyrinth.

And how does a precise and intricate symbol like the labyrinth travel unchanged over such distances and through thousands of years? One of the key

JEFF SAWARD/CAERDROIA

factors is its method of construction—as simple as the design appears complex. A process which, once learnt, allows its faithful reproduction over and over again. And this provides a 'clew' to the universal fascination—a simple test of skill which provides a path for the eye or the feet to follow, an exercise for mind or body. Learn this process and you will be provided with an insight—a map of the path ahead—into the labyrinth that is life itself. More importantly, some will argue, it provides a chance to partake in the unicursal ritual that has survived unchanged for thousands of years: a chance to feel the lure of the labyrinth for yourself.

Not all of this is concerned with the past, for during the last ten years or so the labyrinth symbol and its attendant mythos have undergone a rapid evolution, becoming once again a vibrant concept which has infiltrated into many aspects of public consciousness. The recent upsurge of interest in its history and development has seen a sharing of ideas and information, a bringing together of practitioners and researchers, designers and creators, meeting together

within the 'City of Troy'. At the same time the labyrinth has been appropriated by the media as a theme for computer games, financial chicanery, feature films and television alike. Alongside this is the current resurgence of the labyrinth in its varied multicursal forms as a fundamental part of leisure development, with the construction of many hundreds of mazes, often large and complex, in parks and playgrounds throughout the world.

All of this has created a new recognition of the dual concepts of amusement and amazement. The need for chaos in an ordered, explainable, world has arisen. The temporary suspension of time and direction, an isolation from two of the most important principles by which the world and our life upon it are ruled, has always been attainable within the concealing walls of the labyrinth, be they of tangled yew branches, or of the simple circuitous lines cut into hill-top turf or laid in stones upon the shoreline.

The next episode in labyrinth-time is underway. Welcome aboard!

—*Jeff Saward, February 1991.*

JEFF SAWARD/CAERDROIA

INTRODUCTION

L ABYRINTHS ARE OUTRAGEOUS TOOLS. They can work real magic—moments that bring the different worlds together. Invented in the mists of pre-history by a culture that functioned on quite different levels of consciousness than we do today, these magical single-path mazes enhance the possibility of bringing together our analytical/rational mode of consciousness with our intuitive/spiritual levels of consciousness.

We're living in a time of drastic change—just look at Eastern Europe in the last five years! The ways we do our stuff "just don't seem to be workin' anymore". Our governments are unable to meet the most basic needs of our people—thousands sleep in the streets each night. Wall Street brokers and savings and loan officers are forever developing schemes to part the budding capitalist from his money. (They used to call that stealing.) Scientists have placed themselves in the role of defining truth—ultimate reality—for everyone, and at the same time so many now are aware that the scientist's vision, while quite useful in many ways, "sees" only a small part of ultimate reality.

The Gnostics were a group of Christians who individually sought to experience the other-than-physical realms. Their name comes from gnoscere—"to know" in Latin. The early Church Fathers—who were busy establishing a pyramidal form of Church governance that ended with the Pope on top as the sole human representative on Earth licensed to speak for God—had difficulty with a "cult" where all members exercised that right. The Gnostics "gnew" that there was more than just this physical world because each of them had experienced other realms personally. "To Gnow" means to consciously apprehend the truth/reality of something on *both* the intuitive *and* the rational sides of our being.

More and more people today also gnow that there is more to this world than the reality that mechanistic science has fostered in all of us. There are various terms used to describe how this awareness begins. The one I usually use is "waking up". I feel I woke up in the early seventies when I had a very close awareness of what I would now call The Great Mystery—the One. "Born again" is another term some use. There are others. Whatever term you may use, this other consciousness, this intuitive and deeply spiritual One is sought by many.

Dowsing was my way in. It was the key I used to enter sacred space initially. While this tool of the intuition has usually been associated with finding drinking water, more and more folks have been discovering that dowsing is a way of finding out answers to all kinds of things. I have used dowsing to find out more about sacred space. In this twenty-year study of ancient sacred spaces I have peered back into that time just before history—it was at that time when whole civilizations still seemed involved with the construction and use of sacred space—to places where many experienced the reality of the spiritual realms. Labyrinths are such spaces.

The Hopi Indians, who use labyrinths today, and people in ancient sacred places from Stonehenge and Avebury in England, through the Mayan pyramids and the effigy figures of the Ohio and Mississippi River Valleys, to the Parthenon of the Greeks, the Great Pyramid of the Egyptians and the labyrinth of Crete, were all interested in things like the four directions (North, East, South and West), the Sun and Moon, and Nature. These were seen as part of the Mysteries. They are holy. To honor that, I capitalize all of these directional words throughout the book.

At various points, you will need several different colored pens and a pencil. To make the dowsing tools used in this book, you will need two all-wire coat hangers, and a pair of wire-cutting pliers. If you are not the first to read this book, you might also need some paper. Please don't cheat yourself by not doing the exercises in the "Lessons in Gnowing" at the end of most chapters. You'll miss the point completely if you don't do them. The kind of gnowing that this book seeks to foster is both intuitive *and* rational. It comes from a point of balance between the two.

There are some very good books that give the historical data of labyrinths—where they are, pictures of them, who built them when, etc. 1991 is the Year of the Maze in Great Britain. I suspect that quite a few new books will be on the market as a result of this significant event. (Again, see the Bibliography.) I felt what was needed was a book on the labyrinth's ancient and mythic past, and its potential practical uses to-

day—the two ends of the spectrum. Can the myths tell us something about how these magical mazes were used? They certainly seem to. Also, I have found that labyrinths are excellent holistic problem solvers. They give you a multiplicity of ways of looking at the problem, and then open you up to some intuitively generated solutions, and finally they provide a way of checking out these solutions in a grounded fashion—a way of gnowing.

One last thing: these skills don't last unless they are used on a regular basis. Find ways of using labyrinths and/or dowsing in your life. Build one on your lawn—they don't take up much space, and they are true pieces of Earth art. Find ways of using your dowsing every day.

But most of all, get into that intuition of yours. Develop ways of accessing it on a conscious level. I *gnow* you can do it, and as I suggested at the beginning, labyrinths are a wonderful way to get going.

—*Sig Lonegren, 18 October 1990,*
Samhain New Moon

JEFF SAWARD/CAERDROIA

CHAPTER ONE

SACRED SPACE

THIS IS A BOOK ABOUT INTUITION: and how you can improve it by using it in harmony with the rational side of your consciousness. Labyrinths, which are sacred spaces, are marvellous tools to help you find new ways of developing your intuition. But first, what is a sacred space, and what were they originally used for?

Sacred space is a place where one can go to get help in contacting non-physical realms. Among others, these can be places of emotion, intuition and of the spirit. Whether one is speaking of Stonehenge, a holy well, the Great Pyramid, a Native American Medicine Wheel, Solomon's Temple, a Japanese pagoda, or a labyrinth, this is the case. They are located and designed to enhance the possibility of the supplicant contacting (sometimes very specific) spiritual realms.

There are various components that go in to the makeup of sacred space. While many natural sacred spaces—like Ayers Rock in Australia or Mount Fujiyama in Japan—are basically unshaped by human hands, the holy structures we humans have built on similar power centers in the past all seem to have several things in common. By the use of geometry, the spaces were tuned (like a musical instrument), so they would resonate at a frequency that helped the supplicant connect with the spiritual. Different shapes and internal ratios created unique vibrations that allowed the supplicant to resonate with specific non-physical activities like healing, foretelling the future, or connecting with the One. Most of these sites were also oriented towards a heavenly body like the Sun or the Moon rise or set on a particular day like the Solstices or Equinoxes. This orientation told the supplicant when the site would be at its maximum potential.

All the Earth is sacred; however, there are certain places where the Earth energies come together, where it is easier for us humans to contact the spiritual realms. Our foremothers and fathers knew this and located their temples on Earth energy power centers, places where the active *and* the receptive energies of the Earth came together. If God/dess wants to talk with us, it can happen in the middle of Times Square, Piccadilly Circus, or on the road to Damascus. If we want to communicate with the God/dess, we need all the help we can get. This is what sacred space is all about.

Sacred Geometry

A very special kind of geometry, called "sacred geometry", was utilized in the construction of these places. Any circular structure, like a stone circle or a Native American Medicine Wheel, uses a ratio called pi (π), which has a value of approximately 3.1416. It is the ratio of the circumference of any circle to its diameter—about 3.1416:1. Pi is in a class of numbers called "irrational" in that this number never resolves itself—it goes on forever. Many irrational numbers very quickly fall into a repetitive pattern ($^1/_3$ = .33333..., $^{37}/_{22}$ = 1.681818...), but there is a special class of irrational numbers that never forms a pattern—you can never see a cycle. If you have done the division to figure out the ninety-ninth number after the decimal point in pi, you still have to do the division to figure out the one-hundredth number—there is no pattern. So, with pi, we're working with a number of infinite length (therefore irrational), but also with no apparent pattern. This special class of irrational numbers like pi is called "transcendental", and these numbers form the backbone of sacred geometry.

Another transcendental number is found in the square. If the side is one, the diagonal is $\sqrt{2}$ (1.4142135...). Remember $a^2+b^2=c^2$? $1^2+1^2=c^2$ (or the diagonal of the square), so $1+1=c^2$, or $c=\sqrt{2}$.

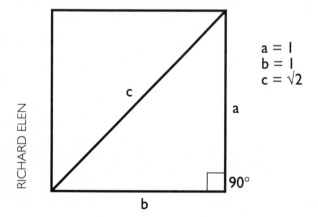

$$a = 1$$
$$b = 1$$
$$c = \sqrt{2}$$

$$c$$
$$a$$
$$90°$$
$$b$$

RICHARD ELEN

1. *The square root of two as found in the diagonal of a square.*

One more example. Both the King's Chamber of the Great Pyramid, and the Holy Place in Solomon's Temple were double squares. They were twice as long as they were wide. This 2:1 ratio is found in Western music in the octave. With a double square, if the shorter side is one and the longer two, the diagonal of the double square is the square root of 5 (2.2360...), a transcendental number. The square roots of two (the diagonal of a square), three and five (the diagonal of a double square) are all transcendental numbers, and they are all found in the construction of sacred space. The ancients wanted to put their bodies in spaces created with the use of transcendental numbers as they represented energies that could assist them in contacting the Transcendent—the spiritual realms. Because unlike other irrational numbers (like .3333...), transcendental numbers (like pi) cannot be known in their entirety, and they have no exact end, or termination point—they don't totally exist in the physical world. There is no *exact* measurement for the diagonal of a double square. So if you want to take your consciousness to a place that doesn't exist on the physical (i.e. the spiritual), why not put your body at, say, the center of a double square—at the intersection of two lines that don't quite exist?

Archaeoastronomy

Most pre-Protestant Reformation sacred spaces North of the Tropic of Cancer were oriented either towards one of the four cardinal points on the compass, or towards some significant astronomical event, usually horizonal, like the Summer Solstice Sunrise, or the Major Standstill of the Moon (an important point on an 18.67-year lunar cycle). This interest of our forefathers and mothers in astronomy is called "archaeoastronomy" (*archaeo* = ancient). Between the Tropics of Cancer and Capricorn, some of the sacred spaces have holes in their roofs to pick up the energy of the noon Sun on the day(s) when it is directly above them. This does not happen outside of the tropics. In the USA or Britain at noon, the Sun is never directly above—it's always at an angle towards the South. In any event, these alignments at sacred sites told the participants when the energy at that particular place would be at its highest.

The Earth Energies

What energy am I talking about? More and more books are being written about peculiar energies that are found around ancient holy places. Many of them mention 'leys'—perfectly straight alignments of ancient holy places. Dowsers have found that sometimes, there is an energy that runs concurrently with these leys, or alignments of holy places, appropriately called 'energy leys'. These six to eight foot wide beams of energy run in absolutely straight lines and have a yang charge. Their yin counterpart is found whenever these energy leys cross. Under these crossings—and under all sacred sites that mark the leys—is underground water. These places where the yang and the yin, the energy leys and underground water, come together are called power centers. They are found in all truly sacred spaces.

I have been investigating the Earth energies that are found at these sacred spaces for over twenty years. One of the major problems students of this energy have is that often different people see it differently. And since the "expert" sees it differently, what others have seen is "wrong". This way of looking at it is very unsatisfactory. Each dowser, each clairvoyant, each

spiritual pilgrim brings their specific level of consciousness and expectations to the experience, and each experiences it in slightly or significantly different ways.

Having said this, one of the ways that many (but not all) dowsers "see" these energies is in the two forms I spoke of earlier: underground water that is yin or receptive, and energy leys—straight beams of yang/active energy that sometimes run concurrently with ley lines—absolutely straight alignments of ancient sacred sites.

Labyrinths

As I want to stress the intuition-enhancing aspects of labyrinths in this book, I will not be focusing on sacred geometry, archaeoastronomy or the Earth energies; however, ancient labyrinths, magical single path mazes, fulfill all of these three characteristics.

JEFF SAWARD/CAERDROIA

2. A Circular Classical Seven-Circuit Labyrinth

Labyrinths come in different shapes from the circular ones of the Scandinavians to the square Classical Seven Circuit Labyrinths of the Hopi of the South-Western United States. There is also a form of geometry in the order of the paths in the classical labyrinths. We will see more of it later at Chartres Cathedral in France, where the geometry is even more clear.

In Sweden, where there are numerous prehistoric labyrinths, many of the oldest ones seem to have an orientation towards the Summer Solstice Sunset. In Gothic Cathedrals, the orientation of labyrinths on their floors (usually in the nave) and the major axis of the cathedral itself are one and the same. Many of these sacred spaces were oriented towards the rising Sun on the particular Saint's day after which the cathedral was named.

Like their other sacred space counterparts, ancient labyrinths were located on power centers. The best examples of this that I have dowsed are found in Sweden, and we will look at this in depth later in this book, but they correspond amazingly well with the Earth energies.

The purpose of sacred space is to enhance the possibility that the supplicant will contact the non-physical, the non-rational. Labyrinths are excellent tools to aid the seeker not only in contacting the numinous, but also in helping the intuitive side of the seeker's being to come to the fore. It is the goal of this book not only to look at the ancient myths about labyrinths to give us a better understanding as to how they may have been used, but also to give some suggestions as to how these magical single path mazes can be utilized today.

Other Enhancers

I have chosen to focus on three aspects of sacred space which are found universally around the Earth in cultures ranging from as early as 4000 BC, for example at the New Grange chambered cairn in Ireland, to the Gothic Cathedrals of the Middle Ages (1300 AD). There are some very pleasant exceptions more recently than that, but in general, Western Man, at least, stopped constructing sacred space by the beginning of the Renaissance.

There are other enhancers of the spiritual quest in addition to sacred space. For example the Medieval Christians developed a way of making stained glass that we've forgotten. This glass allowed only certain frequencies of light to enter the church, and these specific vibrations enhanced the possibility of consciously achieving that Oneness that so many pilgrims sought. Their Gregorian Chants also enhanced this pursuit, with various scales or modes enhancing different spiritual goals.

In other cultures, repetitive dance, drumming, and psychedelic drugs have been used to achieve these results. Incense aids spiritual awareness as well, but while these enhance the possibility of achieving spiritual awareness, they do not bear directly on the issue of sacred space.

Cromwell

If there was such a thing as sacred space, places on this Earth that helped us to contact the intuitive and the spiritual, why didn't we learn about them in school? Why have we forgotten about them? For the last several hundred years, rationalism, humanism, and scientific methodology have been on the ascendancy.

By the middle of the seventeenth century, it was clear to many Europeans that the Catholic and Anglican Churches had forgotten what much of their basic purpose and ritual was about. The Church had been too involved in secular affairs. Humanism called for a placing of the focus on man, not on God.

The death knell of sacred space was delivered by Oliver Cromwell. There was a growing antagonism against the conspicuous displays of church regalia and ceremony that just didn't have any known meaning any more. The Puritans felt that one didn't need to have beautiful pictures or dramatic sculpture or magnificent structures to gain oneness with God. Cromwell allowed his men to enter these sacred spaces on their horses, and did not mind when these horses discharged their bowels on the floors of these ancient holy places. The space was no longer considered sacred. It was what was inside each human that counted in the spiritual quest. The space where that took place meant nothing. It was at that time that labyrinths also began to fall into disuse in Europe, and only small remnants of them remain for us to learn from today.

CHAPTER TWO

THE FORM

MOST MAZES ARE JUST GAMES. Like the Hampton Court maze, or the hedge maze at Longleat, both in Britain, they have many paths, and are meant to confuse, to baffle. They offer too many choices, and the walker of these puzzles is never sure which way to go as there are purposely no clews at points where the path diverges. These mazes are meant to be exercises for the analytical left brain. "Have I been at this point on the maze before? Yes? Then I must take the other path this time." They are artificial mysteries. Games.

A labyrinth is a magical unicursal (single path) maze. It is magical in that through the conscious use of the labyrinth, answers to questions can come, spiritual awareness can be enhanced, the path ahead, in the confusion of the labyrinth's convoluted path, can somehow (magically?) become very clear. It's your choice to enter the labyrinth, but once you have, there is only one way to go—back and forth, back and forth until you ultimately reach your goal—the treasure at the center. All labyrinths are mazes, but not all mazes are labyrinths.

There is a labyrinth pecked out on a rock in Val Camonica in Italy that has been variously dated to somewhere between 1000 and 1800 BC, and a tablet from Pylos in Southern Greece from around 1200 BC. The earliest dated labyrinths are from Cretan coins of around 500 BC. It's this particular Classical Labyrinth that we will be dealing with for much of this book. Many variations have been conceived of since that time. We'll look at some of them as well.

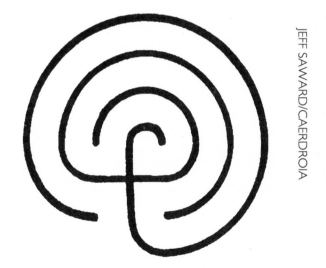

JEFF SAWARD/CAERDROIA

3. Classical Three Circuit Labyrinth

Drawing a labyrinth is really quite simple. Start with a cross with dots in the center of each of the four quadrants:

4. The Basic Form Of the Classical Labyrinth

Now start at the top of the cross, and with your pencil, draw a loop either up and to the left to the dot on the upper left hand quadrant, or up and to the right to the dot in the upper right hand quadrant. For the sake of this exercise, we'll go up and to the right:

5. Building the Classical Labyrinth—Loop One

Then from the corresponding dot in the left quadrant to the right hand end of the horizontal line:

6. Loops Two and Three

And from the end of that horizontal line around to the dot in the lower right-hand quadrant:

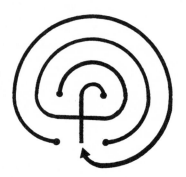

7. Basic Classical Labyrinth (left-handed)

And finally, from the dot in the bottom left-hand quadrant all the way around to the bottom of the vertical line. This is called a left-handed labyrinth because the first turn as you walk in is to the left. If your first move in drawing it had been up and to the left, you would have created a right-handed labyrinth.

Please make three of these left-handed Classical Labyrinths. Draw right in this book on the forms provided at various points throughout. If you are the second or third to read this book, I urge you to get pencil and paper, and draw the simple forms yourself. **Please get a pencil—and, if necessary, some paper—now.**

Thanks. It's really important for you to make the labyrinth with your hand as well as with your mind. You'll "gnow"—know both rationally and intuitively—why later. Suddenly you'll just feel it. Please make three left-handed labyrinths now (first line, starting from the top of the cross goes up and to the right):

JEFF SAWARD/CAERDROIA

8. Basic Building Blocks for Three Classical Labyrinths

Congratulations! Now you know how to draw a labyrinth. There's something very special about making a labyrinth yourself. It happens the fifth or sixth time you make one. It's really quite easy to understand how to make one intellectually once you know the secret, but after you draw it half a dozen times your hand stops knowing how to draw one, and starts *gnowing* how to do it. For this reason, throughout the book will be opportunities to draw many more of them. Please take these opportunities because it will help you to understand these magical unicursal mazes in ways that will not be open to you if all you do is read, or even just think about them. It's another way of knowing.

Back To the Basics: Some Terms

There are some basic labyrinth terms that you need to know. The entrance is called the **mouth**. You walk on the **path**. The path is delineated and con-

tained by the **walls**. The labyrinths you've drawn so far have three paths that finally lead to the **goal**. These paths are numbered starting with the outside path as number one, and ascending inward towards the goal, which in this example, is numbered four:

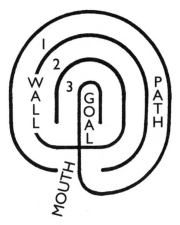

9. Names of Labyrinth parts.

Nasca

It's dry down there on the San José Pampa, near the town of Nasca in South-Western Peru. It's one of the driest places on the face of this Earth. It rains only half an inch every two years. Around five-hundred years after the death of Jesus, before the Incas, at the time when the Mayan civilization in the Yucatan peninsula of Southern Mexico was nearing its zenith, in this parched corner of Peru, the amazing and industrious Nascan civilization was at its peak. The Nascans had constructed marvellous aqueducts that brought water from high in the Andes mountains—many miles to the East. These aqueducts are still in use today, and the water turns what otherwise is a parched desert into lush intensely cultivated farms. The Nascan people made the most colorful pottery in all of Peru. Their clay bowls and dishes were decorated with all kinds of designs and animals. But while the animals on their pottery are well worth the journey down there to see, it is the enormous animals and other forms carved out on the floor of the pampa that have created the most interest.

It's flat. Real flat. While there are mountains or even higher plateaux going up on all sides, at 500 feet above sea level, the Pampa San José is a perfect Sacred Earth artist's canvas. The surface is pure white gypsum, but because of the paucity of rain, the conditions are ideal for desert varnish—manganese, concentrated by various microbial life forms, covering the entire surface of the chalk white pampa with a reddish-brown varnish. In order to paint on this canvas, the Nascans merely had to remove the top layer of varnish. This can be done easily with a broom.

And that's just what they did. There are lines all over the place that come together, like spokes of different widths on a wheel, at hubs, called ray centers. So, if you can imagine, the entire pampa is dotted with these slightly raised ray centers with their straight lines going out and coming in. Some go out to other ray centers, and other lines go out into the desert and just peter out—some at smaller mounds.

One of the first writers to popularize Nasca and the San José Pampa was Erich von Däniken in his book *Chariots of the Gods*. He felt that Earth had been visited by superior life forms from other solar systems, and that the rectangular patches that are also on the pampa along with the lines and ray centers were landing strips for their alien spacecraft.

In addition to the straight lines and the rectangular "landing fields" for von Däniken's flying saucers, there are a series of animal and other shapes that are each made with just one single line. I was down there with Anthony Aveni, an archaeoastronomer from Colgate University, one of the most published authors in the field of pre-Columbian astronomy. Also with me were Gary Burton, a gifted anthropologist from Colgate, and Tom Zuidema, an anthropologist from the University of Illinois who had rediscovered the *ceque* system in Cusco. *Ceques* are straight lines or paths that have holy places called *huacas* along them. At Cusco, 41 of these lines come together at a place called the Coricancha, the Temple of the Sun. It was the major Inca temple in their capital city. In Britain these *ceques* would be called leys, or ley lines, as they follow exactly the definition of leys given to us by Alfred Watkins in the 1920's in his book, *The Old Straight Track*. Ley lines are alignments of holy sites. *Ceques* are leys.

While it was the lines, and their potential astronomical significance that had initially brought me down there, it was the single line animals and other odd shapes that ultimately captured my imagination. One of the figures on the Pampa is a mirror image of the Classical Three Circuit Labyrinth!

Compared to most of the figures and shapes out there on the waterless pampa, the Nasca Classical Three Circuit Labyrinth is quite small, only 15 yards or so across. It's a mirror. The line marks the path rather than the walls, so you walk the line. Also, there is an escape route directly out from the goal. We will see more of this escape route modification later:

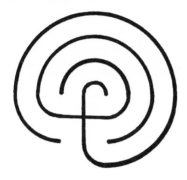

10a. Classical Three Circuit Labyrinth

10b. The Nasca Classical Three Circuit Labyrinth

There are all kinds of animals depicted in the desert canvas—a hummingbird, a thunderbird, a lizard that is over 700 feet long (and is unfortunately split by the Pan American Highway), a pelican, a shark, a dog, to name just some of them. Tom Zuidema calls them "labyrinthine figures"—magical unicursal figures. They are totems or power animals. Many so called "primitive" societies use totemic animals. For example, one might take the eagle as a power animal to be able to soar to great heights, and to see great distances. Someone else might take the bear as their totem to

gain ferociousness. The labyrinthine totemic animals at Nasca were walked in a ritual way to gain, or to take on, the power of that particular animal.

Two of these totemic animals, the spider and the monkey, have particular significance to me. The spider has the usual complement of eight legs, four on each side. The line that makes the 45-yard-long arachnid comes in, or begins, (analogous to the mouth of the Classical Labyrinth) at the next-to-last leg on the right-hand side of the spider, and then goes round outlining this eight-legged insect with its round abdomen and its various legs and head with its eight foot long jaws. It goes back along the two front legs on the right hand side, and out the other side of the same leg you walk in on. This spider has been identified with one that lives on the other side of the Andes Mountains from Nasca. The female spider of this species carries her eggs only on one particular leg—a fact that was only ascertained in this century with the use of a microscope. Would you care to guess which leg it was? You guessed it—the next to last on the right hand side. By walking this labyrinth with intent, you can pick up the energy of the spider—a strong power animal all over the Americas—and you enter and exit the labyrinth/spider at a point which focuses on fertility, reproduction, and continuation of the species.

monkey at its rectum, or root chakra. For the sake of this discussion, let's take the left-hand path.

11b. The Nasca Monkey

This leads up and back from the end of the monkey's spine to form a spiralling tail of just over four turns to the center, and then turns around and goes outward to form its back. The line continues up to the head and arms (one hand has five fingers and the other has four), down the belly to the two feet (each with three toes) and out the root chakra of the animal, on a line parallel to the incoming one. Like the spider, this monkey is not indigenous to Nasca, but comes from the opposite end of the country, up in the mountains of North-Eastern Peru.

Spirals like the monkey's tail are found in many parts of the desert that encroaches on the town of Nasca. One that I was particularly interested in was at

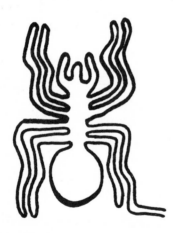

11a. The Nasca Spider

The monkey is another interesting one. It is over eighty yards long, just a bit less than the length of a football field. You begin your labyrinthine walk of the monkey along one of two parallel lines entering the

a place called Cantalloc, just South of town. On a small pampa there were four figures that Maria Reiche, the grand old lady (wise woman) of the Nasca lines, calls "Needle and Thread". Maria Reiche was born in Germany, and has been working on the Nasca figures since just after World War II. She has done more to save these fragile figures and lines from destruction than anyone, and has devoted most of her life to re-sweeping the lines and researching them. I had the honor of going with her to the Needle and Thread at Cantalloc. It has a long isosceles triangle, cleared out like von Däniken's landing strips out on the Pampa San José. At the tip of this 1000 yard long needle, a path zigzags its way thirteen times along the shank of the needle. Each of the four needles and thread at Cantalloc are located on long narrow mesas—like fingers coming out from a hand. The turns on the zigzags were at the edge of the narrow mesas, bouncing back and forth, from side to side. As a dowser, I found water in the form of crossing underground veins of water at each of the V-shaped corners of the zigzagging path. Like the 180° turns on the labyrinth, these water-marked turns on the path symbolize turning points, places to drop burdens. The inside of these crossings were often marked with small piles of stone.

Roughly at the eye of the needle, the zigzagging path turns into a spiral with slightly more than five turns. Like its monkey tail counterpart, it then turns on itself and goes out again, only to be lost somewhere under the needle.

There are some who claim that this zigzag path and spiral form a kind of ceremonial race path. By running that specific path, the runner came to gnow something on the spiritual level. Other cultures run labyrinths. (Kids naturally run them.)

Ohio

This needle and thread pattern is also found up in the United States in Adams County, Ohio, at the Adena Indians' celebrated Serpent Mound. Like the ones in Cantalloc, Peru, it was constructed in about 500 AD, also sticks out on a promontory, and is basically a serpent with (perhaps) an egg in its mouth. More important, like the thread, it zigzags (seven times) back towards its tail, coming close each time to the edge of the narrow promontory. Once again, my dowsing shows there to be water under each turn of the serpent's body. At its tail, it goes in to a tight $1\frac{1}{2}$ turn spiral, like the eye of the needle in Peru.

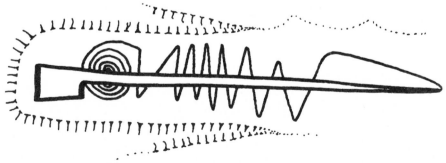

12. Needle and Thread in Cantalloc near Nasca

JEFF SAWARD/CAERDROIA

The Cantalloc Needle and Thread and the Serpent Mound in Ohio were built at approximately the same time. Both are zigzags and have spiral-shaped figures. Both conform closely to the promontories on which they are found. The zigzags, in both cases, are over underground veins of water. Both figures are out at the pointed end of the promontory, and terminate in spirals.

While there are a lot of coincidences here that cause these two distant sites to seem to be related, actually, it's not my intent to convince you one way or the other. The thing to see here is, while they don't look like the Classical ones, all of these figures are examples of labyrinths—magical unicursal paths.

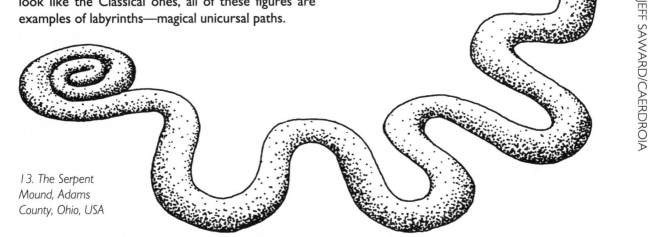

13. The Serpent Mound, Adams County, Ohio, USA

JEFF SAWARD/CAERDROIA

Classical Seven Circuit Labyrinth

The Classical Seven Circuit Labyrinth is the form of a single pathed magical maze that is used most widely around the world. It is based on the cross and four dots of the Classical Three Circuit Labyrinth. However there is one difference. In the Classical Seven Circuit Labyrinth, four right angles ("L's") have been inserted, one between each right angle of the cross and its corresponding dot:

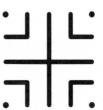

14. The Classical Seven Circuit Labyrinth—The Basic Form

15. *The Classical Seven Circuit Labyrinth*

Just like with the cross and dots, you start at the top of the cross, go up and to the right, only, this time, the line ends at the top of the "L" in the upper right-hand quadrant. Let your hand flow to the left to pick up the next starting point, in this case, the top of the ⌐ in the upper left-hand quadrant, then draw on round to the dot in the upper right-hand quadrant, and so on—see Fig. 15.

JEFF SAWARD/CAERDROIA

Please try it yourself three times, in the space below. How many paths (not counting the goal) does it have?

Labyrinths are found all over the world. While they don't all follow the Classical Labyrinth form, they are all magical unicursal mazes. The O'odham (Papago) Indians of the American South-West have weavings and pottery painted with drawings of what they call "The Man In the Maze".

While the turns initially angle inward towards the center, it is essentially identical in basic construction to the Classical Seven Circuit Labyrinth.

16. Classical Seven Circuit Labyrinth basic forms

JEFF SAWARD/CAERDROIA

17a. Classical (right-handed) Seven Circuit Labyrinth

17b. Man In The Maze (O'odham)

The Hopi

Frank Waters, in his work, *Book Of the Hopi,* talks about the labyrinths of the Hopi:

> The whole myth and meaning of the Emergence is expressed by one symbol known to the Hopis as the Mother Earth symbol. There are two forms, the square and the circular.
>
> There are one circular and five square symbols ranging from four to six inches in diameter carved on a rock just south of Oraibi (a Hopi village in Northern Arizona), and one circular form about nine inches in diameter carved on a rock south of Shipaulovi. A combination of the two forms is also carved on a wooden stick which is planted in front of the One Horn altar in the Kwani *kiva* at Walpi during the Wuwuchim ceremony.
>
> The symbol is commonly known as *Tapu'at [Mother and Child].* The square type represents spiritual rebirth from one world to the succeeding one, as symbolized by the Emergence itself. In this drawing the straight line emerging from the entrance is not connected with the maze. Its two ends symbolize the two stages of life—the unborn child within the womb of Mother Earth, and the child after it is born, the

FRANK WATERS

18. Hopi Mother Earth Symbols

line symbolizing the umbilical cord and the path of Emergence. Turning the drawing so that the line stands vertically, at the top of the page, you will see that the lower end is embraced by the U-shaped arms of the maze. The inside lines represent the fetal membranes which enfold the child within the womb, and the outside lines the mother's arms which hold it later.

The circular type differs slightly in design and meaning. (It is the Classical Seven Circuit Labyrinth.) The center line at the entrance is directly connected with the maze, and the center of the cross it forms symbolizes the Sun Father, the giver of life. Within the maze, lines end at four points. All the lines and passages within the maze form the universal plan of the Creator which man must follow on his Road of Life; and the four points represent the cardinal or directional points embraced within this universal plan of life. "Double security" or rebirth to one who follows the plan is guaranteed, as shown by the same enfoldment of the child by the mother. The additional meaning that this circular type offers is that it also symbolizes the concentric boundaries of the land traditionally claimed by the Hopis, who have secret shrines planted along them. During Wuwuchim and other ceremonies, the priests make four circuits around the village to reclaim this earth ceremonially in accordance with the universal plan.

A structural parallel to this Mother and Child symbol is the *kiva* (the circular underground Hopi sacred space), itself the Earth Mother. The *sipapuni*, the small hole in the floor, represents the womb, the Place of Emergence from the preceding world, and the ladder leading out through the roof for another Emergence to the succeeding world is the umbilical cord. Enactment of the Emergence is given during Wuwuchim, when initiates undergo spiritual rebirth. *(Waters, pp 23 & 24)*

British Turf Mazes

In Britain, they are called turf mazes or Troy Towns. Like the chalk hill figures of England's South, turf mazes need ongoing maintenance to keep them from disappearing. At the Uffington Horse, a chalk hill figure cut into the side of a hill in Oxfordshire, they used to hold a celebration every seven years to re-cut the horse. I have a turf maze in my front lawn, and I can assure you that it needs constant attention. Without maintenance, sooner or later, the grass just takes over. As a result, there are only a few turf mazes left.

Scandinavia

While labyrinths are found all over the world, by far the greatest concentration of them is on the Scandinavian coast of the Baltic Sea and the Bay of Bothnia. Between Sweden and Finland, there are literally hundreds of stone labyrinths. All the ones that I have seen are based on the Classical Labyrinth pattern.

There are many examples of the seven circuit type in Scandinavia. One of the most used ones is the Lindbacke Labyrinth on the edge of the small city of Nyköping, which means "new shopping". Sweden is still rising from the pressure of the last ice age. Since the time of the Vikings, quite a bit of new land has literally risen out of the Baltic Sea.

The Lindbacke Labyrinth was built on the edge of the Baltic. Now the entire new shopping town of Nyköping is between the labyrinth and the sea! I visited this particular Classical Seven Circuit Labyrinth on several occasions with Dan Mattsson, a Swedish dowser, and his son Manfred. It was quite easy to see where the shore had been when it was built, only twenty-five feet from the mouth of the labyrinth. Today, Swedes use it all the time—kids on a school outing, lovers, picnickers, and many others.

The walls of Lindbacke are made of boulders a bit smaller than the average sized head. The overall shape is much like an acorn—rectangular at the end where the mouth is, and circular at the opposite end.

SIG LONEGREN

19a. Dan and Manfred Mattsson walking the Lindbacke Labyrinth

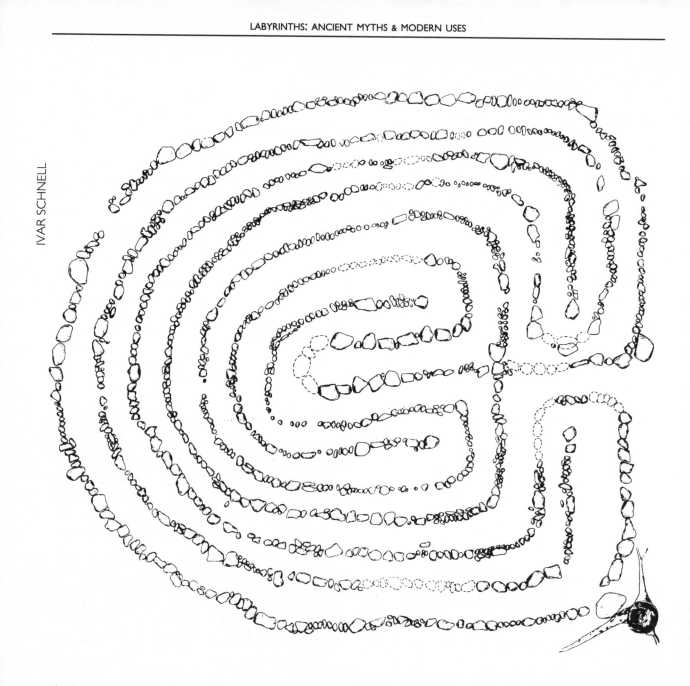

IVAR SCHNELL

19b. Plan of the Lindbacke Labyrinth

Try drawing this acorn-shaped Classical Seven Circuit Labyrinth:

The Scandinavians have taken the Classical Seven Circuit Labyrinth several steps further. Visby is a thirteenth century walled-city on Gotland, an island off the South-East coast of Sweden out in the Baltic Sea. During its heyday, Visby was a center of trade for all of Northern Europe.

Just north of the city is Galgberget, or Gallows Hill, which is honeycombed with tunnels (actually much of Gotland is honeycombed with natural tunnels). At the base of the hill, within sight of the Baltic, is one of the best preserved of Sweden's labyrinths, called Galgberget.

It is an expanded form of the Classical Seven Circuit Labyrinth. Instead of one "L" in each of the quadrants, there are two. The result is called a Classical Eleven Circuit Labyrinth.

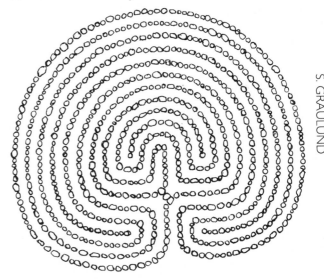

S. GRAULUND

21. Galgberget, Visby, Gotland, Sweden.
The Classical Eleven Circuit Labyrinth. The basic form uses two "L's" in each corner. Notice that Galgberget is a right-handed labyrinth (first turn is to the right).

20. Two Classical Seven Circuit Labyrinth basic building blocks

Try making a few of these yourself. The process is the same. Start at the top of the cross, and this time, *go up and to the left* (counterclockwise) to the top of the first ⌟ in the top left-hand quadrant. Then lift your pencil, and go over to the top of the innermost "L" in the upper right-hand quadrant. Loop over your first line to the top of the second ⌟ in the upper left-hand quadrant. And so on...

Tibble

Perhaps the most exciting stone complex that I saw in Sweden was centered around a tall truncated human-made hill West of Stockholm at a place called Anundshög, near Västerås in Västmanland. At the base of this impressive hill are two large ship settings (*skeppssättning*). They look similar to the stone rings

22. Two Basic forms of the Classical Eleven Circuit Labyrinth (with two "L's"). Try making right-handed labyrinths—first line from the top of the cross is up and to the left.

23a. Plan of the Tibble Labyrinth at Anundshög near Västerås, Sweden.

JOHN KRAFT

of Britain, but instead of being circular, they are shaped like the Viking ships, *vesica*-shaped. A *vesica* is formed when two circles (usually of the same size) intersect. The vesica is only that part of the circles which intersect. In addition at Anundshög, there is a long stone row, various smaller burial mounds, and an impressively tall rune stone.

When a glacier retreats, at times it leaves long piles of gravel. These glacial moraines point in the direction of the retreat (usually in a Northerly direction). For labyrinth seekers at Anundshög, the feast is at the southern end of a nearby glacial moraine. (Most of the earlier Swedish labyrinths are found at the southern end of similar moraines.) This one, called Tibble, is certainly part of the Anundshög complex and is the most complicated Classical Labyrinth I've seen. It has three "L's" in each quadrant! The turf has grown up since it was built, and some of the stones are under the surface. John Kraft worked out the plan on the prev ious page by probing the stones with a thin iron rod. It is a Classical Fifteen Circuit Labyrinth:

23b. The Classical Fifteen Circuit Labyrinth basic building block with three "L's".

Chartres

The Knights Templar, members of a military religious Order of Poor Knights of the Temple of Solomon, was formed during the aftermath of the first Crusade. Established by Hugues de Payns in 1118 for the protection of pilgrims, initially the Templars were a band of nine knights who were quartered beside Solomon's Temple in Jerusalem. Much of their history is surrounded in myth and intrigue, but one thing is certain. Upon their return to Europe, they instigated one of the most innovative and massive architectural campaigns in modern European history, the Gothic Cathedrals.

Many Gothic Cathedrals initially had labyrinths in them. Unfortunately, for various reasons, many of these labyrinths have been removed. Fortunately, there is one in particular that has remained relatively unscathed. It is found in Chartres Cathedral, just West of Paris, in France. Chartres, built on an earlier pagan site, dominates the countryside around it. It is the result of massive dedication on the part of the people of that area, and was built in only twenty-nine years.

The magnificent labyrinth is found in the nave of that majestic cathedral. (Most cathedrals are laid out like a cross. If you imagine the rather grisly image of someone hanging on that shape, the nave is the long bottom part of the vertical line, the bottom of the body. As you walk down the nave towards the High Altar at the other end of the cathedral, the labyrinth is at the thighs, and when you come to the outstretched arms, this vertical line is the transept. Where the head would be is the choir and the High Altar.)

In astrology, each sign of the zodiac rules a portion of the body. Aries rules the head, Taurus the neck, Gemini the lungs and neck, and so on down the body. The thighs are ruled by Sagittarius which corresponds to the long journeys and pilgrimages we take in our lives. The Chartres labyrinth is for pilgrims—many of whom did that labyrinthine journey on their knees. Try walking the white path of the labyrinth with your eyes.

24. Chartres Labyrinth.
Can you walk the white path with your eyes?

Perhaps you're familiar with the magnificent stained glass rose window that is directly above the main door of the nave at Chartres. It is the same distance above the floor as the labyrinth is down the nave from the front door. This circular rose window and the Chartres Labyrinth are the same size. If you could imagine there being a hinge at the end of the nave where the main doors are, and if you could fold the front facade down towards the altar, the rose window would lie directly on top of, and would be congruent with, the labyrinth. The light of that famous window, and the darkness of the pilgrimage are one.

As with the Classical Seven Circuit Labyrinth, we will talk more about the potential uses of the Chartres labyrinth later on. For the moment, please notice that it is divided up into four obvious quarters, and that each of these quarters has seven 180° turns. If you counted them correctly, there are also seven paths on the Classical Seven Circuit Labyrinth.

In this book, I have only used illustrations of labyrinths that I have personally seen. Obviously, there are many more dotted all over the Earth. In China, as early as 1000 AD, rectangular labyrinths made of incense were used to measure time. Each straight length of incense took a known amount of time to burn, so in a ceremony, for example, as the incense came to a corner, the celebrant knew it was time to get on to the next part of the ritual. Egypt has the oldest known maze, built around 1795 BC by the Pharaoh Amenemhat III of the XII Dynasty. First identified by that great antiquarian and Egyptologist Flinders Petrie in 1888, it is located near the town of Bellet Caroon, south of Lake Moeris. This nightmare of choice was 1,000 feet from East to West by 800 feet from North to South. It was enormous with many, many rooms, (according to tradition it had between 1,500 to 3,000 above ground, and 1,500 below ground), but it wasn't a labyrinth. There were literally hundreds of choices one had to make as one worked one's way through this early maze.

There are many other places where labyrinths can be found, from the walls of Pompeii in Italy to the Hollywood Stone in Ireland; from a Roman-type labyrinth in Turkey to Zulu mazes in Africa.

It is not the intent of this book to cover the whereabouts, geography and age of all the labyrinths in the world. Rather, we will work with ancient myths and modern uses. The point I want to make here is that labyrinths, magical unicursal paths, are found pretty much all over the world. There are several good books dealing with where they are, their history, and who might have built them. See the Bibliography at the end of this book. What I want to explore in depth in the rest of the book are the earliest stories about them which might give us a hint as to how we can use labyrinths, these magical tools of sacred space, today.

Mirrors

In this chapter we have talked about various magical unicursal paths, focusing on the Classical Labyrinth and how to make it. In the process we have looked at labyrinths in various parts of the world with specific examples in North and South America, and in Europe and Scandinavia. The Classical Labyrinth in its various forms is found in all of these places, but in different forms. It is these diverse forms that are fascinating to me. They lead the seeker into mirror after mirror. The left-hand labyrinth mirrors the right-handed ones. (Draw one on a plain piece of paper with a dark pen. Determine whether it is a left or right handed labyrinth. Now turn the paper over and hold it up to the light. *Voilà*! The mirror!

The Nascan Classical Three Circuit Labyrinth is a mirror to most of the other labyrinths. On the Classical Three Circuit Labyrinth, the path is in between the lines/wall. At Nasca the path becomes the line, and the walls disappear. Another mirror!

This shifting back and forth, this positive and negative, this Light and Dark, is part of what labyrinths are all about. Psychics and others who travel in other non-physical realms like the astral world report that polarities are switched. Left becomes right. Future becomes past. In dowsing the chakras, I find that their polarities shift alternately as I move up the spine from the root chakra to the crown. Mirrors represent these shifts. Labyrinths help the individual make them.

Lessons in Gnowing

At the end of each chapter there will be exercises designed to help you 'gnow' more about these ancient spiritual tools. Remember, gnowing is a combination of both—opening up to the intuitive, but also using your rational faculties. At this time, the most important exercise is to keep on drawing Classical Seven Circuit Labyrinths—the ones with one "L" in each quadrant. Please use the Basic Forms opposite to make three left-handed (up from the top of the cross and to the right) Classical Seven Circuit Labyrinths. Please remember, if someone has already drawn in this book, make your own forms and labyrinths!

25. *Classical Seven Circuit Labyrinth basic forms*

CHAPTER THREE

THE MYTH

MYTH IS NOT HISTORY. It is not truth. And yet it points to truths far beyond historical "fact". Myth serves to explain some aspect of the human or natural world or of the spiritual realms beyond the five senses, beyond the rational mind. It speaks of the times before written history. Frequently myths speak in archetypes—the hero, Goddess, the ruler of the underworld, the shadow, the messenger. These archetypes are also found inside each one of us, and through the awareness of the way they work in myth, we can come to a greater understanding of ourselves.

I suspect that no myth is told exactly the same way twice: each teller adds part of his or her own essence to the tale. Sometimes cultures, for purposes of their own, change significant portions of a given myth; however, the essential bones of the story seem to carry through the many tellings and revisions.

Myth is important to the study of labyrinths because it can perhaps lead us to the truth behind the truth, a glimpse of the initial meaning and use of these amazing unicursal magical tools. So here is my version of the story of the most famous labyrinth of all, the Minoan Labyrinth of Crete that held the Minotaur, and of the hero Theseus, the most renowned of the Greek mortals:

Theseus and the Labyrinth: A Myth In Five Scenes

Scene one: Athens

Theseus was the most famous mortal hero of the Greeks. More stories about his many exploits were handed down to us than of any other human Greek superstar of that era. Actually, I want to tell you about only a small portion of his life when he got mixed up (or rather when he didn't get mixed up) in the Minoan Labyrinth.

Born of Aegeus, King of Athens, and Aethra, the daughter of one of his friends, Pittheus, Theseus grew up with his mother in a town called Troizen. His father had left his sword and a pair of his sandals under an enormous boulder, and told Aethra that when Theseus was big enough to move the stone, he should take the sandals and sword, and follow his father to Athens. That day finally came, and after many adventures, mostly with robbers and bandits—whom Theseus defeated handily—he arrived in Athens. It was an obvious foretaste of heroic deeds to come.

Medea, Jason's love in his quest for the golden fleece, and the tragic figure of Euripides' famous play, was, at that time, Aegeus' wife and had borne a son by him. She did not want this new and unexpected claimant to the throne to interfere with her own machinations to hold the power in Athens.

Theseus did not immediately announce himself to his father. Medea took advantage of this blind spot, and told the king that the young man who had recently arrived in Athens having killed all kinds of bandits on his way, was really an assassin, and urged the king to poison him. Aegeus agreed, and invited the assassin to a banquet in his home. Medea slipped the poison in Theseus' banquet cup. A giant roast was brought in to the room. Just as they were about to drink a toast to the roast, Theseus most gallantly offered his sword to the king to cut the roast. His father, recognizing the sword, knew its holder was his son, and knocked the poison cup out of Theseus' hands. Exit Medea, stage left.

Scene Two: Crete

Minos was the King of Crete and ruler of the Minoan civilization. Its capital was Knossos. Early in his kingship, at a time when things had not been going too well, Minos had asked Poseidon, King of the Sea, to give him something suitable to offer to the gods. It would be a sign that the gods were with him. "What you give will be returned again to you."

Poseidon sent a white bull charging out of the sea—sleek, full of beauty and perfection. Minos immediately coveted this creature of heavenly origins. It was so flawless that he decided to keep it for his own herds, and to sacrifice another of his bulls instead.

Poseidon, of course, was miffed. It never pays to oppose the gods.

Poseidon caused King Minos' wife, Pasiphaë, to become totally enamoured with the white bull. The Queen became so infatuated with this animal that she found herself driven by the desire to mate with this divine gift of masculine tumescence.

At that time in Knossos there lived a very skilled Greek named Daedalus. He could do many things, and was said to have introduced the Minoan civilization to both the plumb bob and the augur. He was also the most respected architect in Knossos. Pasiphaë went to Daedalus and pleaded with him to invent some kind of structure on which she could consummate her ever increasing passion for the bull. Daedalus designed a full-sized model of a cow in which Pasiphaë placed herself. It was rolled into the field where the white bull was kept, and she was thus finally pacified.

The result of this unnatural union was a monster—half man and half bull—the Minotaur (Minos + Taurus). He turned out to be such a horrible and unmanageable beast that Minos had Daedalus build a labyrinth to keep him in. It was a maze, full of dead ends and false turns. If anyone was foolish enough to wander in to this maze, they would never find their way out, and ultimately they would be found by that monster of the darkness, the Minotaur, and devoured.

Prior to the Minotaur, Pasiphaë had borne her husband King Minos four children. All but one were to have tragic ends. Catreus was killed by his own son. Phaedra, made famous by the French 17th century playwright, Racine, died by her own hand. Ariadne was another daughter of whom we'll hear more later. Androgeus, another son, was sent by Minos as an emissary to Athens several decades before Theseus had arrived there. Foolishly, the Athenians had allowed Androgeus to meet the Bull of Marathon. It killed Androgeus.

In other versions, the Bull of Marathon was the bull which Theseus slew after his return to Athens. In any event, some bull from Marathon gored him to death. King Minos, in retaliation, demanded that once every nine years Athens send him seven of their best men and seven of their best women—the cream of the crop. And it was time for the third batch of Greek youth to be sent to the Minotaur just when Theseus was reconciled with his father.

Who would be chosen this time?

Scene Three: The Journey

"Send me to Crete as one of the seven men," was Theseus' response.

One can just hear Aegeus' reply, "I can't send you, Theseus, you are the next King of Athens. These are sacrifices we're sending."

"Father, send me."

"Look, I just won't allow it."

"Send me."

Theseus' persistence finally won the day, and with much sadness, the funeral barge was prepared with the black sails of mourning. Aegeus told his son that if he were to return successfully, he should signal this by using the white sails that were packed under the floorboards of the barge. With that, Theseus set off with the thirteen other young Athenians for Knossos.

Naturally, Minos wanted to show off his Greek sacrificial victims to the people of Crete. He set up games where the victims competed with the Cretans. In one, Theseus found himself wrestling a giant of a man who was Crete's best wrestler. As any good hero should have, Theseus deftly trounced him. When he was presented with a garland of flowers for his victory, he looked round the cheering throngs, and his eyes met Ariadne, Minos' daughter. He walked up to her and gave her the flowers. (Enter Eros, stage right.)

Scene Four: The Clew

Now the idea here was that these Greek youths were to be offered, one at a time, to the Minotaur. One by one, they would be led to the mouth of the labyrinth, from which they would descend to their inevitable doom. Ariadne knew this, and her growing love for Theseus, like her mother's love for Poseidon's white bull before her, led her to the home of that inventive Greek, Daedalus. He had created the labyrinth. He held the key. After some tearful persuasion, Daedalus yielded, and told her to bring a ball of twine to the mouth of the labyrinth and tie one end of it at the mouth. Several versions that I've heard say that the next thing was to put the ball on the ground, and it would roll to the center and the Minotaur's lair.

Ariadne ran to give this clew to her love, Theseus. Late that night, Theseus did just what Daedalus suggested. He took the ball of yarn that Ariadne had given him to the mouth of the labyrinth. It didn't need to be guarded, because nobody ever entered that hell-mouth and returned alive. Theseus carefully tied one end of the ball of yarn to the lintel of the door of the mouth, put the ball on the floor, and began his descent after it. He finally came upon the Minotaur, who was asleep in his foul bed at the center of the labyrinth. With the element of surprise in his favor, and with his tremendous strength, Theseus killed the monster with his bare hands.

He then picked up the ball of yarn, and retraced his steps out to Ariadne, who was waiting for him at the mouth of the labyrinth. Together they freed the other Greeks, raced back to the boat, and beat a hasty retreat back towards Athens—some say, not before putting big holes in the bottoms of all the Minoan ships to foil pursuit.

Scene Five: Forgetful Theseus!

The first island that they landed on after their flight from Crete was Delos, the most holy isle of the Greeks, birthplace of both Apollo and Artemis. There they danced the Crane Dance in celebration of their escape. It is said that this was the first time ever that men danced with women. This Crane Dance is done to this day on Delos, and in it, the dancers follow the path of Theseus' descent into the labyrinth.

Their next port of call was Naxos, where some say Theseus intentionally left Ariadne; others say he forgot her. Others still speak of a dream he had in which Dionysus told him to leave her there. Take your pick, he ditched her, and sailed for Athens without her. He also "forgot" to change the sails from black to white. Aegeus, standing on the cliffs looking for the boat's return, saw the black sails, and thinking that Theseus was dead, leapt to his death in sorrow. The Aegean Sea is named after him. Theseus landed in Greece to find he was now King of Athens and from there went on to many more exploits.

Curtain calls: Epilogue

Daedalus and Icarus

King Minos was no fool (except when it came to keeping promises made to the gods). He knew that there was only one way Theseus could have known how to get in and then out of the labyrinth. Daedalus must have given him the clew, the thread. So he imprisoned Daedalus, and his son Icarus, in the labyrinth. You know the next part. That old inventor Daedalus figured out how to put bird's feathers on to frames, and after warning his son not to fly too close to the Sun, they took off across the Aegean.

Do kids ever listen to their parents? No, they never listen, and Icarus was no exception.

But the story doesn't end with Icarus' premature plunge from the heavens and his father's safe landing on another island. No. Having been cheated again, Minos wanted revenge. It was said that Minos went from island to island trying to catch him by making an offer he knew Daedalus couldn't resist. At each island, Minos went to the local king with one of those spiralling shells that had a small hole punched in the small end. Minos said he would give a lot of money to someone who could figure out how to get a thread strung from the bigger opening to the smaller.

Minos finally came to the island of Sicily, where the local king was indeed protecting Daedalus. Intrigued, the king brought the problem to him. Daedalus couldn't resist. He tied an ant to the thread, stuffed it through the small hole at the small end, and smeared honey all over the mouth at the big end. The ant went for the honey, dragging the thread after it. When the local king showed it to Minos, the crafty Cretan knew that Daedalus was on the island, but the local king wouldn't give him up, so Minos left empty-handed.

The White Bull

After he had experienced the pleasures of Pasiphaë, no cow of the royal herd could satisfy (dare I say pacify?) the white bull. It went berserk, and ran amok all over the island of Crete. No fence could hold him, and hunting parties proved unsuccessful in tracking him down. Animal passions gone amuck. The containment of this white bull later became one of the twelve labors of Hercules. After a fierce struggle, this famous Greek hero brought the bull back in fetters.

Ariadne

Left to her own devices on the island of Naxos by Theseus, Ariadne eventually met Dionysus, the last of the Greek pantheon of gods to be installed, and the first to be attacked and removed. They fell in love and lived together. They are said to have had a wonderful marriage. When she died, she was deified and Dionysus gave her a place in the heavens: the constellation Corona Borealis, or the Northern Crown. (Interestingly enough, the Native Americans call this same cluster of stars the spider, who spins her own kind of labyrinthine web.)

26. Ariadne/The Spider/Corona Borealis/The Northern Crown

Theseus

Continuing on his path of being the most written-about Athenian mythological hero, after his return to Athens and Kingship, Theseus captured the Amazonian Queen Antiope for his first bride. He also reclaimed the Marathonian bull that had killed Minos' son Androgeus and started all the labyrinthine troubles for Athens in the first place.

Among his many other exploits, the one that is most germane to the story of the Cretan Labyrinth is that after the death of Antiope, Theseus' second bride was none other than Phaedra, Ariadne's sister! (Her father, Minos, tried to warn her, but did she listen?) After their marriage, Phaedra fell in love with Hippolytus, son of Theseus and his first wife, Antiope. Hippolytus refused Phaedra's advances, so to spite him, she told Theseus that his son had tried to have intercourse with her! Theseus called down Poseidon's wrath who frightened the young man's horse with a tidal wave, and Hippolytus was then dragged to his death. In sorrow Phaedra hanged herself. Theseus learned too late of his mistake.

He went into Hades in an unsuccessful attempt to rescue Persephone, and escaped only with the help of Hercules. As a mortal, he not only breached the gates of Hades, but he could communicate with the gods. Theseus was, indeed, a very talented mortal who could go to, and work in, very different realms.

In his old age, Theseus gave up his kingship and retired to Skyros where he was treacherously murdered by King Lycomedes. His father's nemesis, Minos, ended up in the underworld with his brother Rhadamanthys, as a judge of the dead. In Hades, Rhadamanthys judged the Asiatics, and Minos was the pagan St. Peter for the Europeans.

Helen of Troy

There is another Greek myth that we shall later see ties in quite interestingly with the labyrinth, and this is the myth of Helen of Troy. While I don't want to go in to the whole story that was the subject of Homer's *Iliad* and the Roman Virgil's *Aeneid*, it is interesting to note that, like Minos of Knossos, the Trojans' problems began when they insulted Poseidon. In their case, they were building a great wall around their city. It was so great that it was necessary to

DIANA GRIFFITHS

evoke divine aid for its construction. Poseidon agreed to assist them; however, he also told them that he wanted to be compensated for his assistance.

When the wall was finished, it was so massive and apparently impenetrable that the Trojans didn't feel it necessary to show Poseidon proper respect and gratitude for his help. Poseidon withdrew his protection, and the city became vulnerable to attack. For this miscalculation, Poseidon supported the Greeks in the ensuing war.

In the 12th century BC, after the time of Theseus and the Minotaur, according to Greek tradition, Paris, a son of King Priam of Troy, kidnapped Helen, wife of the Greek King Menelaus of Sparta. The chieftains and nobles of Greece got together under Agamemnon, and went off to Troy. They fought the Trojans for over ten years! Beautiful Helen, whose face it has been said launched a thousand ships, stayed with Paris till the end of the war when she was captured by the Greeks and brought back home with her husband, King Menelaus.

The Goddess in the Center

This isn't even a myth. There's no story. Only an unusual and persistent theme in both Finland, Sweden, and we'll see later, in England as well, of a girl or woman in the center of the labyrinth. According to John Kraft, Swedish labyrinth expert, there are numerous stories of specific labyrinths where a woman stood in the center, and then others danced towards her, or in some cases, men raced to her in order to dance with her, or if he could get in and carry her out with no mistakes, if he was successful, the girl would be his.

We spoke earlier of the Classical Eleven Circuit Labyrinth on the Swedish island of Gotland called Galgberget, or Gallows Hill. There is a myth connected with that labyrinth that says it was built by a woman who was being held prisoner there. Each day she brought one large stone to build the circle. On the day she brought the last stone, she was released.

So we have stories of women held prisoner at the center of the labyrinth, of a woman who caused a great walled city to fall, and of the monster that Theseus slew at the center of that Cretan Labyrinth.

Interpretation Number One

One way of looking at these myths is that the prison guards, the warriors who cunningly brought that white horse to the Trojans, and that Greek hero Theseus, all represent what has come to be known as the patriarchy, a male-centered, analytical, power-motivated, rational mode of operation.

The woman in the center, in both the Trojan and the Minoan civilizations, represented final holdouts of an earlier Goddess-centered religion. Indo-European concepts had obviously influenced both cities. Troy, with Poseidon's help, had just built "impregnable" walls. Knossos had the best navy in the world. Both fell to this new male skill called "cunning". To others, it is deceit.

Many authors today speak of evidence of a more feminine-centered religion that held sway in the Eastern Mediterranean before the introduction of the patriarchal monotheistic God of the Light and of the high places. Jehovah and Allah are two of the names patriarchal people call their Gods today. The God of Men. (Oh yes, and of course women too.)

While one could spend a lot of time speculating as

to what that time was like before single male deity archetypes took over the Eastern Mediterranean, the relatively small part of the world where Moslems, Jews and Christians trace their spiritual roots to today, one thing seems clear. Before the entrance of these male deities into the Eastern Mediterranean, the Goddess in all her forms held a much more important role. Written history has not done Her justice. This Goddess religion was eaten away by the ever-increasing incursions of the Indo-European ideas that more and more people in that part of the world were converting to. In Greece, these barbaric patriarchs, the Ionians, the Achaeans, and finally the Dorians, invaded that country from 2500 to 1000 BC. In Troy and in Knossos the matrifocal influence was for a while kept alive after the Goddess had been suppressed in Greece and in the House of Israel.

One of the things that you will have noticed by reading the Theseus myth is that the Minotaur couldn't have been kept in what we are calling the Classical Seven, Eleven or even Fifteen Circuit Labyrinth. No one could be so stupid as to need a string to find their way out! It's impossible to get physically lost. Walk to the center in one direction, kill the Minotaur, and walk the way you came in in reverse. You don't need a string. The Minotaur must have been kept in a very complicated maze—not a labyrinth.

The modern experts on labyrinths are insistent on its being one single (unicursal) line—not a series of choices that Theseus had to make. At the beginning of this chapter I said that no myth is told exactly the same way twice, each teller adds his or her own flavor to the tale.

Sometimes cultures, for purposes of their own, even change significant portions of a given myth. Perhaps this contradiction in terms is evidence that this is really a much earlier Minoan story that the Greeks adapted to their own use. Perhaps when they were rewriting the tale to suit their own need to demonstrate their superiority over the Minoan civilization, they used the word "labyrinth" instead of "maze" because that was the word used in the earlier Minoan myth, but they had forgotten about the magical aspects of this unicursal sacred space. Keep this contradiction in mind.

Lessons In Gnowing

The important thing is for you to continue to draw the Classical Seven Circuit Labyrinth. Your hand needs to gnow what to do. To gnow what sacred geometry is all about, you need to understand it in some other way than just through your rational mind.

On the following page are three more Classical Seven Circuit Labyrinth basic building blocks. This time, try to make them as quickly as possible. Try to feel the flow. You will maybe find that you don't need to think so much as you construct them. Your hand will begin to gnow what to do.

27. *Classical Seven Circuit Labyrinth building blocks*

CHAPTER FOUR

THE DREAM

"In archaic art, the labyrinth—home of the child-consuming Minotaur—was represented in the figure of the spiral." (Joseph Campbell, The Masks of God, Vol. I: Primitive Mythology.*)*

DREAMS ARE MESSAGES. Almost everyone has experienced dreams that feel significant. Sometimes these are repeating childhood dreams, or recurring themes like going on stage and not knowing your lines, or sitting for an examination and not even knowing the title of the course, let alone the answers to the questions. Sometimes they are nightmares. But what do they mean? Stories as far back as the Old Testament tell of rulers and others who are unable to interpret their dreams, and of the power that was given to those who could.

Jung and the Myth

In this century, it was the psychologist Carl Jung who brought the interpretation of dreams into scientific acceptability. Jung had an abiding passion for gnosticism: indeed, a portion of the Nag Hammadi Documents, the Jung Codex—consisting of about fifty papyri—is located at the Jung Foundation in Zürich. Ultimately, Jung, as a good gnostic, would argue that each of us must decipher our own dreams. We need to gnow what they mean. By all means, listen to what others may have to say, but remember, ultimately it is what they mean to *us* that is important, not what someone else thinks.

Jung's map of the psyche, the whole human being,

serves as a useful model for many different thought systems that have come after him as an overlay of their particular areas of interest for the individual's return to wholeness. In the tradition of the gnostics, it empowers the individual, not the therapist—who follows the client's lead.

Myths are human truths on the symbolic level that can be treated as dreams. In fact, Jung obtained a portion of his concept of the archetypes, the symbolic figures of our collective unconscious, from the myths of the Greek Gods and Goddesses. So, dear reader, let us look at the story of the Cretan Labyrinth as if it were a dream to see what it might tell us about this magical tool:

Poseidon was the ruler of the sea, the unconscious. If you think of yourself as an enormous iceberg, that part of you that sticks out of the water is your consciousness, your self-identity. Poseidon rules that seven-eighths of the ice that is below the surface of the water. Poseidon was offended by Minos' refusal to sacrifice the white bull as he had promised. The unconscious thwarted will have its way. In retribution, Poseidon set the stage for an unnatural act to occur that united the energy of the god/archetype/unconscious with the physical human.

In other mythologies, there is talk of the "Sons of

God". In the Old Testament we are told, "when men began to multiply on the face of the ground, and daughters were born to them, the sons of God saw that the daughters of men were fair; and they took to wife such of them as they chose." (*Genesis* 6:1 & 2)

The traditions and legends of the people of the Republic of Georgia at the Eastern end of the Black Sea say that Sons of God came to rescue them from the giants who ruled the Earth. (*Genesis* 6 also speaks of these giants, the Nephilim). The Georgians prayed to the heavens for help, and the Sons of God came down on a golden chain to save them.

Usually the stories at least imply that these meetings brought forth benefits to humanity and to the Earth. The result of this particular union between the White Bull of Poseidon and Queen Pasiphaë was a monster—an abomination called the Minotaur. This animal was nothing to emulate.

Of Tunnels and Shadows

The Old Testament talks about half-human half-animals. Ezekiel had a vision where he went up into the Temple and found himself in the Holy Of Holies, the most sacred room of the Temple—in Solomon's time, the spot where the Ark of the Covenant was kept. In this room, he found a door that led down into a tunnel: under the Earth again. It's amazing how many ancient places of sanctity had tunnels associated with them: Solomon's Temple, the Hall of Records at the Great Pyramid, and at Machu Picchu—an Incan stronghold hidden in the vastness of the Peruvian Andes, where tunnels have recently been discovered. Irish *fogous* are basically a series of tunnels, and of course Glastonbury Tor, one of Southern England's most sacred pilgrimage sites, has legendary

tunnels running under it. Lots of other sacred spaces around the Earth have these tunnels, or at least stories about underground passages.

When Ezekiel descended into his tunnel, he found all kinds of elders of the house of Israel down there secretly worshipping in the darkness. "Portrayed upon the wall round about, were all kinds of creeping things, and loathsome beasts, and all the idols of the house of Israel." (see *Ezekiel* 8) The serpent worshippers in their "room of pictures" created abominations, monsters of the deep, half animal half human, minotaurs.

The Cretan Minotaur was also a big embarrassment to the royal family. The beast had to be kept from public view. This black monster born of lust and illicit passion had to be kept in the dark. These dark deep secrets that we put down in the deeper recesses of our being, hopefully never to see the day, are called by Jungians our "shadow". According to Jung, the shadow is the "us" that we repress, that part of ourselves that we don't like, and don't want to deal with. The Centaur had a horse's body and a human head. The most famous Centaur, Chiron, was known as a wise teacher of Hercules, Jason, Achilles, and Asclepius. His human nature ruled his animal passions. On the other hand, the Minotaur had a human body and a bull's head. He was ruled by his animal nature. The shadow represents our animal instincts inherited in our evolution from lower life forms. It contains sexual and aggressive impulses which cannot be approved by the conscious ego. In dreams, the shadow figure generally appears as the same sex as the dreamer.

Minos put the Minotaur, the keeper of shadows, in the labyrinth.

Theseus

Then along comes Theseus, one of the archetypal human heroes of the next age who stood for patriarchal ideals—might makes right, logic over intuition, and above all, male rule. More stories were written about Theseus than any other human in Greek mythology. He became King of Athens upon his return to that city. He stood for the Light. He acted with cunning and courage with the clew, and with duplicity towards Ariadne. But more of that later. What Theseus did was to go bravely down into the labyrinth, and kill his shadow. In killing the shadow, Theseus became a role model for that which stood in opposition to the cthonic Mother Goddess of the Darkness. Plato, in *The Cave*, talked about shadows on the wall that were basically poor reflectors of "reality". This emphasis on the Light produced a corresponding pejorative attitude towards the Darkness. (Notice how seldom you see that word capitalized, and how often the word Light is?)

The Anima

Ariadne was played for a sucker. Theseus not only got the clew from her that saved his life and the lives of his friends, but then he ditched her almost immediately thereafter. Ariadne did it all for love. When Theseus gave her his victory bouquet, something happened inside her. It caused her to take actions that certainly permanently messed up her relationship with her family. She did it for love. If Theseus is this dream's ego, and the Minotaur is the shadow, Ariadne becomes the Jungian *anima*, the female counterpart to the male dream ego. In this dream, she was only a means to someone else's end, and yet she was the one who had

that vital clew. She had the secret of the labyrinth.

Fortunately mythology deals well with this mistreated and used woman. On Naxos, the island that Theseus ditched her on, Ariadne met Dionysus, god of mysteries and of the grape, they fell in love, and had a perfect marriage.

Patriarchs *vs* Goddess

So, let's look at this myth as if it were a dream of the meeting of the patriarchal assertive Greek consciousness with the more Goddess-oriented Minoan Civilization. Our hero, and the dream ego, is a Greek. Like the modern boxer's dream, he was undefeated in the various physical scraps he found himself in. He proved that before arriving at his father's palace, when he cleared the road to Athens of all of the brigands and other nefarious miscreants. Theseus went to Knossos in response to Minos' son, Androgeus, a symbol of the Minoan state of ambivalence at that time. Theseus was willing to fight his father's war—a war that he had absolutely nothing to do with starting. Theseus hadn't been in the picture when Androgeus was gored by the Bull of Marathon.

Minos ruled a civilization where Goddess was still seen openly and clearly. Goddess worship there wasn't total, She was in her decline (Minos did have the world's best navy and could still extract tribute from Greece), but unlike the more patriarchal civilizations around Crete like Greece and Palestine, the Minoans still held feminine energy in high esteem. This was symbolized by the fading feminine Crete sending Androgeus (androgyny) to the rising patriarchs of Greece. Unlike Theseus, Androgeus wasn't up to the task he found before him. He was killed by the Greek bull, a well-rooted vision of masculine animal energy that was taking over that part of the Eastern Mediterranean in the second millennium before Christ.

A more probable version of the death of Androgeus is that the city-state in Greece called Marathon had an unusually strong supply of ferocious bulls, and they put forward their best each year. Androgeus, Theseus and Hercules all fought different bulls of Marathon. This choosing of your best to sacrifice to the Gods is an important theme in this myth. Athens' seven best young men and women were the ones that were sent to Crete. It is precisely due to this one that Minos got in trouble. He did not offer his best bull to Poseidon. He kept that white bull from the sea for himself and gave Poseidon his second best, with disastrous results.

In any event, Theseus, the dream ego sets sail, across the sea, the unconscious, to destroy the Minotaur, his arch-nemesis. In his heroic defeat of the giant Cretan wrestler, Theseus gains the love of Ariadne, his anima (or feminine counterpart to his male dream ego). He uses this opening to his advantage, using her in the process.

The hero really uses this female for his own ends. This woman—one of the best known females in Minoan history and mythology—is treated with literal abandon. First, she gets him the clew by going to Daedalus, who represents the archetype of the new kind of consciousness that was coming in, the left brained scientific inventor, to whom Cretan women turned when they didn't know what to do. (His Greek mind, on the other hand, *does* know what to do.) Secondly, one way or another, Theseus ditched Ariadne, who was apparently no longer useful, on the island of Naxos.

Western Man's Shadow

But I get ahead of myself. The point of this voyage/dream/myth for Theseus was to make it so Athens didn't have to send the cream of its youth to Crete as meals for the Minotaur. The way to stop this was to remove the appetite. Theseus went to this monster, his shadow, all of those dark things that Greece didn't want to look at, feed, or deal with—and slew it. As a result, Western Man hasn't had to look at his shadow again—until this century when Carl Jung began talking about it so persuasively.

Everyone has stuff they don't want to deal with. The Greek Gods always had trouble with their women. They wouldn't behave like the Gods wanted them to. And on the island of Crete, where there was still a great deal of open worshipping of Goddess in the Minoan Civilization, we have a monster who is neither God nor mortal. And the Greeks were having trouble with it. This fusion of the unconscious, the God Poseidon, and the more animal instincts of the human female Queen Pasiphaë, seems to be symbolically saying, "We Greeks no longer wish to travel to our unconscious to face those dark things in our lives that we'd rather forget."

Now, Jung suggests that the way to deal with your shadow is to meet it directly head on. The unconscious will meet us with the same kind of energy that we bring to considering it. If we run from it, it will chase us. But by looking at those pieces of your stuff that you've ignored for years, one by one, they will cease to hang around your neck as a dark weight. The way one works with the shadow is with bravery and with loving acceptance. One must meet the shadow head on and incorporate it, bring it back into consciousness. This is not to say that you must take on the characteristics of your shadow and manifest them, but you need to consciously repossess these repressed parts of yourself.

Now how did this myth's dream ego deal with his shadow, this major monster in his life? He cunningly snuck down to the bowels of the labyrinth at night, when the foul beast was sleeping. Theseus, this archetype of the heroic Western Man, sprung on his shadow, and slew it. No incorporating going on here!

So the shadow has been slain. The dream ego and his anima—and his brother and sister sacrificial victims—escape from the land of the Goddess: but not before cunningly knocking holes in the bottoms of all of the Minoan ships, so that they couldn't be followed.

The Crane Dance

On the island of Delos, they danced the Crane Dance. The steps follow the path of the Classical Seven Circuit Labyrinth. The crane, like the stork, brings life. Many who dance in a chain of people into a labyrinth experience the feeling of being born. As you squeeze through that sea of people, it gives one a feeling reminiscent of what it must have been like to come down that birth canal. According to Robert Graves, author of *The Greek Myths*, this Crane Dance was the foundation of what later became the "Troy Games" where this dance was done. (Haven't we heard of a connection between the labyrinth and Troy somewhere before?)

For me, the hardest thing in writing this chapter has been not to be judgemental about our hero,

Theseus. He is a number one cad. A real schmuck. He destroys his shadow; he leaves his anima on the island of Naxos (thus cutting himself off from his own female side); and he "forgets" to change his sail, thus contributing directly to his father's death. Sure, he killed the Minotaur, but at what cost? The most amazing thing to me is that Theseus got away with it. They made him king, and he is always thought of as one of the good guys in Greek mythology!

Lessons In Gnowing

It is possible to create a labyrinth out of eight concentric circles, but this is a relatively more difficult way to do it. Also, as Joseph Campbell pointed out at the beginning of this chapter, in archaic art, the labyrinth is represented by a spiral. Spirals are found all over megalithic Europe. Perhaps the most famous are found at New Grange, a chambered mound in the Boyne Valley north of Dublin in Ireland. This chamber is dated at least three thousand, if not four thousand years before the birth of Christ. Others are found in Carnac in Brittany, and on all kinds of Greek and Roman pottery. Then, of course, there are the spirals on monkey's and serpent's tails in the New World.

The Classical Seven Circuit Labyrinth is basically an interrupted spiral. But even more to the point, as you draw three more labyrinths on the next page, using the basic Cretan form, notice how you are, in effect, drawing a spiral—you just lift your pencil off the paper occasionally. Try three more of these forms on the following page to see for yourself.

28. *Classical Seven Circuit Labyrinth basic building blocks*

CHAPTER FIVE

HERSTORY
Female Centered Prehistory

"But what is surely clear is that a firm continuum has been established from Lake Baikal to the Pyrenees of a mythology of the mammoth-hunters in which the paramount image was the naked goddess."—Joseph Campbell.

WHEN I WORKED ON MY Master's Degree in Sacred Space in the late seventies, while I briefly studied Paleolithic peoples and earlier (including the Cro-Magnon and Neanderthal), my studies of sacred space began somewhere between 3000 and 3500 BC with such structures as the long barrows like West Kennet, an early part of the Avebury megalithic complex in Wiltshire, New Grange in the Boyne Valley in Ireland, and a bit later, the early pyramids like Saqqara, in Egypt. Two of the most famous European sacred sites, the Great Pyramid and Stonehenge I were at least five-hundred years later. And all of this was very early indeed.

While recalibration of radiocarbon dates and other archaeological dating methods have now pushed the dates of some of the structures mentioned above back to almost 4000 BC, some people are beginning to write with great specificity about a time in Europe several thousand years before that! Feminist writers like Merlin Stone (*When God Was A Woman*, called *The Paradise Papers* in Britain) and Monica Sjöö and Barbara Mor (*The Great Cosmic Mother Of All*) among others have been talking for some years now about that time when the dominant spiritual force in Europe and Asia Minor was Goddess. It was a time that has been denied by many historians and archaeologists. It is a time before history.

As the victors write the history, and feminists, to whom I remain indebted for much of the material presented in this chapter, would argue forcefully that the victors for that last several millennia have been men, history really is *his* story. But we speak of a much earlier time, before the invention of writing (at least as we know it today), before Menes-Narmer, a king of the first dynasty in Egypt (3100 BC) and the earliest person whose name was recorded in history. This was a time two or three thousand years before that. Many are now calling this time before history "herstory".

Marija Gimbutas

One of the most influential authorities on the time before history in Europe is Marija Gimbutas, professor of European archaeology at UCLA (University of California, Los Angeles) and the curator of Old World archaeology at UCLA's Cultural History Museum. In her numerous books she speaks more and more articulately about the time before 5,000 BC in Europe. It was a time when Goddess reigned supreme, a time of peace; the villages she excavated in what she calls "Old Europe" (the Balkans, Greece, Crete, Southern Italy) did not have defensive perimeters or walls. It was a time when sacred spaces were found in the midst of the village in rooms within the home, and in small buildings not set apart from the rest of the community. Metals were in use then, but they were used to make jewellery or agricultural implements; metal was not used to make implements of war.

In an interview in *woman of power*, a remarkable magazine that is a leader in presenting this information in the United States, Gimbutas presents one rather compelling bit of evidence that supports this notion of a Goddess-centered civilization at that time, "When I became a professor at UCLA, I had a chance to start excavations in South-East Europe—in Yugoslavia, Greece and Italy. This way I learned a lot about objects that are found, and I personally found at least five-hundred figurines, at least ninety-five percent of which are female." (*woman of power*, Issue 15, Fall/Winter 1990, p. 7.)

Goddess was/is everywhere—immanent—rather than the transcendental up-in-heaven God of Christianity. Feminist authors speak of the Goddess at that time as being of the Earth, of the dark places, and of the holy well. She is the Mother of us all. Riane Eisler, author of *The Chalice and the Blade* has taken Gimbutas' material, and has concluded that it was a time of peace and creativity, during that time at the very dawn of agriculture. Eisler argues that it wasn't matriarchy—at least in the sense that matriarchy might be seen as the rule of women over men. Women don't naturally work that way, she argues. Rather, they cooperate, and she uses the term *gylany* to describe this form of harmony. "Gy" comes from words like gynecology, geography and Gaia, "l" links "gy" with "an" from andro, "y" is a state of, so gylany is "a state of linking

J. BENNETT

L. WILLIAMS

29. Drawings of Bird Goddess with Meander. Left: Upper Paleolithic Bird Goddess carved with meanders from Mezin on the River Desna in the Ukraine; c. 18,000—15,000 BC. Right: Neolithic and Copper Age meanders mark Bird Goddess figurines like this terracotta duck-masked figurine. Late Vinca; 4500 BC. (From The Language of the Goddess *by Marija Gimbutas, page 26.)*

between the feminine and the masculine".) She then suggests that if indeed there was a time when humans live in peace, and didn't need defensive positions, it is not a genetic given that men are macho and given to "power over" trips. We men *can* act differently. War isn't a necessary given at least every generation or two. This is an encouraging concept for our future.

The Meander and the Labyrinth

Several years ago, Jeff Saward, editor of *Caerdroia*, a magazine dedicated to the study of labyrinths, and a friend of his, Jim Kimmis, were playing about with reducing labyrinth designs to their basic elements, *ie* taking out the lines that simply connect one turn to another.

One day, over a pot of tea and a pack of chocolate biscuits, it came to them—the basic form of the Classical Seven Circuit Labyrinth was the meander, a pattern that is found on thousands of Greek and Roman artifacts!

Named after a river in Turkey that "meanders" to the extreme, it has come to mean aimless wandering, but of course, the meander is anything but aimless.

30. The Meander/Greek Key

Trace your finger between the walls. Doesn't it give you a feeling of aimless wandering? The interesting thing about this meander pattern is that Marija Gimbutas has found it all over Old Europe—five or six thousand years before the Greeks hit their peak. It is one of several themes that seem to come into play in

31. From Meander to Labyrinth (above)
Here is how the meander grows into the Classical Seven Circuit Labyrinth. Hold the book with your thumb on the right edge of this page, at about the same height as this caption. Gently slide your thumb off the edge so as to flip through the pages rapidly. Watch the meander unfold like a fan, to reveal the Classical Seven Circuit Labyrinth—and then fold up back into a meander.

terms of how Goddesses of Old Europe manifest themselves. There are pregnant figurines, the Bird Goddess, the Snake Goddess, the White Goddess of Death, the Pig Goddess ("sow" seeds in the spring), and others.

The Bird goddess is one that seems to be quite relevant here. There are different symbols carved on bird figurines from wavy lines to triangles and lozenges (diamond shapes). Another symbol that is found frequently on ceramic birds of this period is the meander (Fig. 29).

The Bird Goddess also comes to us in the form of the Crane, a water bird with long legs whose migratory flight path takes it over all the places we've been talking about in the North-Eastern Mediterranean—Old Europe.

Gimbutas has found this meandering pattern on what she calls a Bird Goddess figurine found at Mezin, on the River Desna in Western Ukraine datable to some time between 18,000 to 15,000 BC.

This takes us back well in to the time of Joseph Campbell's naked Goddess of the mammoth hunters. The roots of the labyrinth seem to run deep into herstory.

The Trojan Connection

Perhaps one of the most dominant themes in Northern Europe and its labyrinths is the connection with Troy. "Caerdroia" is Welsh for "labyrinth". Literally, *caer* means hill, and *droia* means Troy, and also "to turn"—a pun on the City of Troy/city of turnings. In England, they're "Troytowns" or "The Walls of Troy". The Trojan roots are deep in Britain. According to Geoffrey of Monmouth (1100?-1154), one of that island's earliest historians, in his *History of the Kings of Britain*, the first king of that fair isle was Brutus, son of Virgil's hero Aeneas who left Troy after the Greeks finally breached that city's famous walls. The blood of the first king of Britain came from Troy.

Likewise, the Scandinavians connected the labyrinth with Troy. They call them "Trojeborg", or Troytowns. John Kraft, an expert on the Swedish labyrinths, and author of *The Goddess in the Labyrinth* speaks of the repeating motif of a woman in the center of the labyrinth. At one we have already looked at, the Galgberget Labyrinth, outside of Visby, on the island of Gotland, the story of how it was built is intriguing. Remember the king's daughter who was being held prisoner there? She added one stone every day to the labyrinth. When she finally put all the stones in place (and I assure you there are lots of stones, and some of them are big), she was freed.

Kraft tells another story about a labyrinth on the East coast of Sweden:

"At Köpmanholm in the archipelago north-east of Stockholm an old man told me the following in 1978 of a labyrinth locally known as "Jungfruringen" (Virgin's Ring): As a little child at the beginning of this century he heard from old people how the labyrinth had been used. A girl was placed in the center. After that two boys started a race from the two entrances of this particular figure. Their objective was to reach the girl first. They both had to run the same distance and they met each other in the path somewhere on their way. The one who came first to the centre got the girl." (Kraft 1985 p. 17). See Fig. 32.

At a labyrinth in Saffron Walden in England, a maiden stood at the goal (home) while the young men tried to get to there in record time without stumbling.

What is this Northern European fascination with Troy? How does this theme of a woman (sometimes held prisoner) in the center of the labyrinth fit in?

From a feminist perspective, Troy was a major turning point. You may remember that at the beginning of the story of the Trojan War, the city didn't have any defensive walls. Because of some perceived threat, they found that they needed them, and so they asked Poseidon to help them, with disastrous results. Along with Crete, Troy was one of the last strongholds of the Mother in that part of the world. It was at the very end of what Eisler calls the time of gylany.

But more important, the Trojan War was fought over a woman. Paris, a Trojan prince, convinced Helen to leave her Greek husband and to go with him back to Troy. The response from the Greeks was clear. "Hey woman, once you're married, your place is in the home. Don't go traipsing after someone else, or we'll go to war. And we're willing to stay at war for over ten years to get you back! A woman's place is in the home!"

For the people in Northern Europe, Troy held a key to things of the Mother at a time when the Patriarchy was gaining the upper hand. Labyrinths were/are a way back to Goddess. Walk the path, and find Her in the center. Then what about this *male* beast monster, the Minotaur, in Crete?

JOHN KRAFT

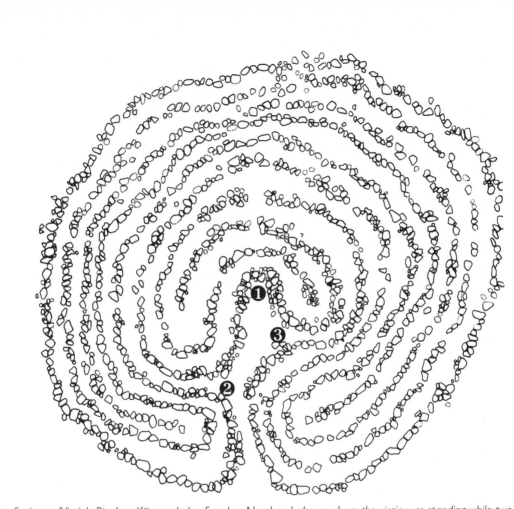

32. The Jungfruringen (Virgin's Ring) at Köpmanholm, Sweden. Number 1 shows where the virgin was standing while two boys stood at 2 and 3. They ran the paths in opposite directions to reach her first. (From The Goddess in the Labyrinth *by John Kraft, p. 18)*

Goddess in Crete

Both King Minos and his wife, Pasiphaë, had divine origins. According to the *Larousse Encyclopedia of Mythology*, "Minos was the son of Europa and Zeus. Europa was the daughter of the King of Phoenicia. She was struck by the beauty of one of her father's bulls."

(that fascination ran in the family didn't it?)

"The bull actually was Zeus in disguise. When she climbed on his back, the bull/Zeus carried Europa to Crete where he raped her.

"Europa gave birth to Minos, Rhadamanthys and Sarpedon. All three were adopted by the King of Crete, Asterius, who subsequently became Europa's husband." (Guirand, 1959. p 111)

In a book entitled *Myths* edited by Alexander Eliot, but perhaps more importantly with contributions by two major modern male pre-historians, Joseph Campbell and Mercea Eliade, the authors talk about the women connected with King Minos. "...Pasiphaë [was the] daughter of Helios (the Sun King) and wife of King Minos of Crete. Pasiphaë and her daughters Ariadne and Phaedra in Greek mythology are figures of tragic love, embodying all the confusion, despair, and madness of that emotion. Pasiphaë was originally a Moon Goddess, represented standing beneath a white cow. *The story of her unnatural passion for the white bull of King Minos was a later development.*" (my italics) (Eliot, 1976, p 193)

The Minotaur As a Replacement

I feel the Minotaur himself is a later development as well. The most famous story of the labyrinth is an aberration. Most of the other labyrinth myths have women in the center, not male monsters. Many of the Greek Myths are stories from much farther back with an essentially patriarchal/Greek overlay. In this case, initially there was a Goddess, Ariadne, in the labyrinth. The Minoan labyrinth on Crete and the City of Troy/Trojeborg once symbolized the same thing.

While Pasiphaë had divine roots as a Moon Goddess, her daughter Ariadne also had once been a deity in her own right. One of her epithets in ancient Crete was "Mistress of the Labyrinth". Christine Downing in her book *Goddess: Mythological Images of the Feminine* speaks of her growing awareness that Ariadne had been much more than a stooge for Theseus. "This Ariadne belongs to an ancient matrilineal period of mother-goddess worship. She is not just a mortal girl who is Theseus' beloved, nor is she just someone made a goddess through her connection to the god Dionysus. She is an immortal in her own being. She is not a mortal who becomes immortal, but an immortal whom later traditions have transformed into a mortal. Ariadne is one of the pre-patriarchal goddesses who blend in and out of each other in confusing ways because they are women in their woman-ness..."

"Ariadne is one of the Great Mothers, a great goddess of Crete. As such she is titled the Potent One, the Mistress of the Labyrinth, the Untouched One. To ask who Ariadne is, to follow the thread all the way to the end, leads us to the center of a labyrinth and at that center we find Ariadne herself." (Downing, 1988 pp 62 & 63)

The design of the labyrinth is much older than the Theseus myth. The meander pattern on which the Classical Seven Circuit Labyrinth is based goes back at least fifteen thousand years before Theseus slew the Minotaur. Most of the characters in the myth, including Daedalus, were Greek, (only Minos and his family were Minoan) and of them, only Ariadne knew how to get into the labyrinth. The myth states that she learned the design from Daedalus, but this appears to be a later detail to "prove" the inventive and mental superiority of the Greeks over the Minoans.

So, in addition to a monster, your shadow, the Minotaur, you can also meet Goddess—your feminine intuitive side who can fill you with ecstasy and an awareness that can only come from a spiritual force that is immanent. The patriarchal Greeks, of course, didn't want to foster that kind of thinking, so they took a much older Minoan story and gave it a new twist—and in the process degraded the feminine and elevated the masculine.

The Labrys

We can see a further piece of this patriarchal takeover if we look at linguistics. There is a tool that is found frequently in the Minoan civilization called a *labrys* (notice the linguistic similarity to labyrinth). The labrys is a double-headed axe, and was found by Sir Arthur Evans in great numbers, inscribed and painted on the walls, when he excavated the palace of King Minos of Crete at Knossos—where the labyrinth was said to be as well. In addition to these inverted double axe-heads, bare-breasted women somersaulting over the very long horns of bulls and fanciful peacocks done in stucco adorned the interior walls of the palace which was grouped around three sides of a central courtyard.

Sir Arthur felt that the Hall of the Double Axe-Heads was important because the labrys was also found in Heinrich Schliemann's Troy, thus showing the Trojan/Cretan connection that keeps coming up again and again. There was apparently a great deal of contact between the two cities.

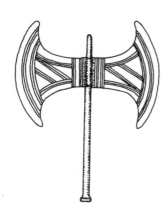

33. *Gold Labrys from Knossos, Crete*

This special axe, said to be used originally by Scythian female warriors as a scepter, was a favorite of the Amazons. It has become one of the modern symbols of women's power and of the Goddess. It is also a very powerful symbol of our time. There seems to be an intimate relationship between Goddess and both the labyrinth and the double-headed axe, the labrys. Neither word was originally Cretan. They came from the South-West Coast of Turkey—from a land called Caria. Caria is where the Meander River reaches the Aegean Sea. Caria was a Greek colony, but "labrys" and "labyrinth" are not Greek words—they come from the earlier (more gylanic) people who lived there, the Caunians, who did not speak an Indo-European language—unlike their Greek conquerors.

The Celts

Let's leave the labrys with the Caunians for a moment, and look at the Celts. Every barbarian that Caesar fought and memorialized in his *Second Gallic War*, (*Gallia est omnis divisa in partes tres...*) was a Celt. From the New Testament Galatians to the Gaelic people of Ireland, most of Iron Age Northern Europe was populated with Celtic/Indo European stock. There are some exceptions to this—the Uralic speaking peoples of Hungary, Latvia, Lithuania, and Finland are not of Celtic origin. The Samii people of what we call Lapland, and the Basques of Southern France and Northern Spain were not Celts (pronounced *Kelts*, unless you're a sports fan, in which case, it's pronounced *Selts*). But most of Iron Age Northern Europe was Celtic.

We can see this evidence of Celts from their writing on many stones in the Iberian peninsula of Spain and Portugal, and the salt mines of Hallstädt, Austria, to the magnificent Gundestrup Cauldron found in a bog in Denmark. The sacred isle of Anglesey, off the North coast of Wales, was the last great stronghold of the Druids (magician-priests of the Celts) in the Roman conquest of Britain up to Hadrian's Wall.

Donal Buchanan has studied linguistics, etymology and codes for much of his life. His studies have shown him that when the Celts came to the Black Sea, they split into two groups, the *Brythonic* and the *Goidelic*. The Brythonic Celts pressed on into Europe, and became the barbarians that Caesar fought in Gaul. Today they are the Celts found in Brittany, Cornwall, and Wales. The Picts of Scotland also had Brythonic roots.

On the other hand, the Goidelic Celts first went South into Turkey. Turkey has always stood at a crossroads of trade and ideas. The Hittites at the end of the third millennium before Christ were another group of Indo-Europeans who got there before the Celts. On their way through that area, the Goidelic Celts met the already patriarchal Greeks, Jews, and Phoenicians. They also met, and apparently intermingled with, scattered tribes like the Caunians who had held on to their matrifocal past.

Some Goidelic Celts stayed in Turkey. The *Book of Galatians* in the Bible speaks about these people. Gaul was in France, Galatia was in central Turkey, they were both Celtic. From Turkey, the Goidelic people went to Egypt where, for a while, they served the Pharaoh. From there, they skipped along the North coast of Africa to the Iberian Peninsula of Spain and Portugal. Buchanan has studied the Goidelic inscriptions in Southern Portugal, and has found clear evi-

dence of their path through there on their way ultimately to Ireland, the Isle of Man, and as the Scotii, into Scotland.

But it was in Portugal that Buchanan discovered an interesting connection with the labrys. The vast majority of the phonetic symbols of this script represent individual consonant or vowel sounds. However, there are a small group of symbols that represent more complex sounds. One of these has the sound of *Con*, and is scribed:

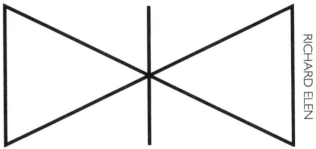

RICHARD ELEN

34. "Con" in South West Iberic Goidelic

Con is the labrys, the sacred double-headed axe of the Goddess, only in Portugal it meant "chief", "reason" (a left brain function), and "dog" or "wolf". In Gaelic, the Irish name "Connors" used to mean "chief". Male chief, reason! The Caunian labrys, in the hands of the Indo-European Goidelic Celts, was patriarchalized —just like the Theseus/Minotaur/Ariadne myth.

Lessons in Gnowing

The Fool

At many of the Earth Mysteries Gatherings and Oak Dragon Camps in England, we build labyrinths. At one, a Summer Solstice Earth Mysteries Camp at the western end of the Mendips—a low ridge of hills in Somerset, North of Glastonbury—we decided to build one on the side of a hill that sloped down towards a beautiful sweat lodge that some other participants had already constructed.

One of the participants at that camp was a man in his thirties who was a computer programmer from London. He obviously had not had much experience in the great outdoors, and had clearly demonstrated that the day before, when we were digging what are delicately called "shit pits". While apparently perfectly willing, this fellow didn't seem to know which end of the shovel to use! He really seemed to be quite ineffective, and I must admit, he made me rather frustrated and angry.

The next day, five or six of us, including the computer programmer from London, gathered on the side of the hill to build a Classical Seven Circuit Labyrinth out of six inch bamboo stakes and string. We began by making the cross, the four "L's", and the four dots. We then made the walls out of more stakes, putting them about eighteen inches apart in ever-increasing arcs. This can be somewhat confusing as you end up with a large number of sticks—about four-hundred or so—in what can seem to be a baffling array. It's important to mark the basic building block with longer sticks at first so you can make some sense out of it. In any event, we got all the sticks in correctly with the usual moment or two of confusion. (This seems to be an absolute necessity when you construct a labyrinth with sticks and string. Just hang in there—muddle through—and you'll get there.)

Then we began to wind the string around the sticks to better delineate the walls. Everyone seemed to get the knack of doing it except the computer fellow from London. He took the string and began to wind it on one stick and then another in a totally random pattern. At first, I thought that he was just confused, and I tried to help him to get it right. It soon became clear that he couldn't get it right. The more I tried, the more confused he apparently became. I thought, "What a fool!" Then I realized that was just what he was—a Fool!

For the rest of the afternoon, he completely filled that archetype. He took off his clothing (clothing is optional at gatherings such as these) and crawled through the labyrinth. Later, when a woman was lying in the center, he ran in, and (with absolutely no sexual energy attached to it), jumped on her. He was a fool. He was *the* Fool.

The next day, I went up to the labyrinth, and found yesterday's Fool standing at the mouth of it in deep contemplation. As I walked up to him, he began telling me about several things he had noticed concerning the layout of the Classical Seven Circuit Labyrinth that I had never been aware of before. First he pointed out that there were seven paths and the goal, and if you number them from the outside path in, that you walked them in the order of: 3-2-1-4-7-6-5-8. Notice that it is a repeating pattern. **3-2-1-4** and **7-6-5-8**. They both offer the same kind of flow—coming down from near to the top down to the bottom, and then springing up to the top. Walk the paths with your finger and feel these numerical changes for yourself:

JEFF SAWARD/CAERDROIA

35. *The Order of Paths—3-2-1-4 / 7-6-5-8*

My "foolish" computer programmer friend from London then began talking about the cross at the heart of the basic building block. He showed me that the first turn you take is (in a left-handed labyrinth) in the lower left quadrant (A), and the final turn is in the upper right quadrant (C). They are the *alpha* and the *omega* and only a dot, an infinitesimally small point in the center of the cross, separates them, and yet you

have to go for such a long distance to get from one to the other. So near and yet so far! The beginning of one's journey, and the end are literally right next to each other.

Also, the other two quadrants of the cross—the upper left (B) and lower right (D)—mark the beginning and the end of path number four: exactly in the middle of one's walk through the labyrinth! So the cross delineates both extremes and the means!

RICHARD ELEN

36. *The Cross. (A) is the first turn, (B & D) mark the middle of the journey, (C) is the last turn before reaching the goal.*

So many times in our history, the Fool has been an important figure. On one level, he is apparently absurd, meaningless, foolish. On the other hand, in medieval courts, the Fool was the only one who could tell the king the truth and get away with it. I have heard it said, "Only the wise man knows he's a Fool". In the case of this labyrinth, the Fool had become my teacher. And what a gift Michael Bloom, for that is his name, had given me! The awareness of the order of the paths (any fool could have seen it, but I hadn't) has given me a much deeper understanding of what this magical tool is all about. In many ways I trace my esoteric awareness of the labyrinth to this experience. We will be working with this 3-2-1-4 / 7-6-5-8 path order in much greater depth later on, but let me give you just one example:

Just as there are seven paths, there are seven notes in our musical scale. To keep things simple, let's use the key of C. Then let's make 1= middle C, 2=D, 3=E, 4=F, 5=G, 6=A, 7=B, 8=C above middle C (one octave up).

This makes the quadrants of the cross make more sense—the *alpha*=C, and the *omega*=C is one octave up. So near, and yet so far—an octave apart.

But more to the point, the order of the paths, gives you the music of the labyrinth! The music goes E D C F / B A G C. (The / is a rest between two similar patterns.) This is really a very pleasant melody line that can be easily built upon to make a very harmonious tune. It can also be hummed as you walk the labyrinth.

If you have a piano, wooden recorder, guitar or other instrument, try playing it. Hear the music of the labyrinth. Play it over and over. Experience the feminine muse of the labyrinth.

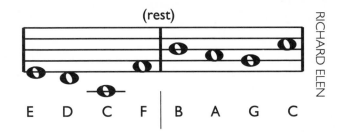

RICHARD ELEN

37. Musical notation of the music of the labyrinth: E-D-C-F / B-A-G-C.

CHAPTER SIX

THE ENERGIES

J UST AS AT ALL OTHER sacred spaces, labyrinths built before the Protestant Reformation—or at least before Western Man's consciousness pervaded the culture that built them—are located on Earth energy power centers, places where yin and yang energies get together. A good acupuncturist doesn't put the needles in anywhere along the meridians, s/he puts them where these two elemental forces come together. This is also true for sacred space. Let's take a look at the yin force first.

Water

Probably one of the best books on the construction of sacred space is the Bible. There are all kinds of instructions on how to build various sacred structures including Noah's Ark, the New Jerusalem, the Ark of the Covenant, and Solomon's Temple. In the last chapters of Ezekiel we have one version of how to construct The Temple (there are two other sets of Temple instructions—in II Chronicles and I Kings). Ezekiel begins Chapter 47 by reporting that "water was issuing from below the threshold of the temple towards the East *[for the temple faced East—the direction of the Equinox Sun rise]*; and the water was flowing down from below the South end of the threshold of the temple, South of the altar."

Holy wells and sacred baths are an integral part of sacred sites all over the world, from the series of sacred baths at Machu Picchu in Peru and the Chalice Well in Glastonbury in Southern England—where many miraculous cures have occurred—to Lourdes in France, the healing center *par excellence*. In Vermont, where I did much of my field work for my Masters degree, there are underground stone chambers that exemplify all three of the topics mentioned above—they were built with sacred geometrical ratios, oriented towards significant horizonal astronomical events, and built on earth energy power centers. At many of these sites, springs and shallow wells play an integral part.

But dowsers, who are best known for their ability to find water, have taken this even further. Many dowsers, starting with European diviners in the nineteen-thirties, find underground water at the very center of sacred sites. This water, from underneath the Black Madonna at Chartres Cathedral, under the altar stone at Stonehenge, at the center of Anasazi *kivas* in New Mexico, comes from an unexpected source. First of all, it doesn't come from the sky. It is brand new water (not recycled through the process of evaporation and rain). It comes from way down in the bowels of (our Mother) the Earth. It is the result and by-product of various chemical processes that take place down there under great pressure and heat. The simplest explanation comes from high-school chemistry. Perhaps you may remember that a base plus an acid yields a salt plus water. Mix sodium hydroxide (lye) plus hydrochloric acid (very nasty stuff), and you get sodium chloride (table/sea salt) plus water. $NaOH + HCl = NaCl + H_2O$. Down in the Earth, all kinds of chemical processes are going on, usually much more complicated than the example given here. In any event, water is the by-product of many of these reactions. And what does water do when put under heat and pressure? It tries to escape, so it goes up towards the surface of the Earth through any crack or crevice it can find. Sometimes this water finds necks, vertical tunnels in the rock that it can shoot upwards through at terrific force. If it reaches the surface, there is a geyser. This doesn't happen in 99.9% of the cases as the neck is sealed off from the surface by some impermeable layer like rock or clay. This neck is called a dome (in Britain, a blind spring). The water then finds smaller cracks at various depths in the neck where it continues out laterally in what dowsers call veins of water. Dowsers find these domes with their veins at many of the more important ancient sacred spaces.

From above they look like a spider with her round body (the neck) and an odd number of legs (the veins). See Fig. 38.

The most interesting thing about these yin Earth Mother energies of domes at sacred spaces is that either the structure conforms to the dome and veins, or the dome conforms to the shape of the sacred structure. (It's a chicken or egg question. I come down on the side that the domes were there first, and the site was constructed in harmony with it.) In Vermont, many of the underground chambers have domes with a diameter exactly the same size as the width of the chamber, and the veins go out of the four corners of the rectangular chamber and out of the mouth. In Ireland, at Cairn T, a neolithic chambered mound at Loughcrew, north-east of Dublin, the dome's story is the same. In this case, there is a cross-shaped tunnel with the single longer arm leading to the mouth of the chamber. The dome is located on, and is the same size as, the crossing. Two veins exit into the back chamber, one each out of the two side chambers, and one vein runs the whole length of the entrance, exiting from the mouth of the chamber. I have dowsed this pattern

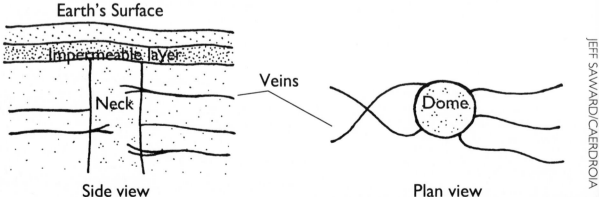

Earth's Surface

Impermeable layer

Neck

Veins

Dome

Side view

Plan view

38. A dome with five veins exiting.

of the structure built in harmony with the underground dome of water again and again at sacred places around the world.

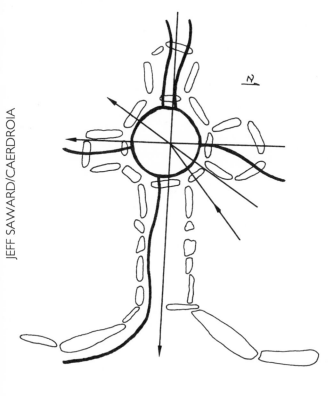

JEFF SAWARD/CAERDROIA

39. Dome at Carn T, Loughcrew, Ireland

Energy Leys

Energy leys represent another form of energy that dowsers find at sacred sites. They are six to eight foot wide beams of yang/active energy that flow in straight lines across the countryside. Often, but by no means always, these energy leys are found to run concurrently with ley lines—the ancient alignments of sacred sites that have now been found on all the continents of the Earth. These energy leys, like their yin counterparts, the domes and veins of water, conform to the layout of the particular sacred space. For example, one energy ley is usually found running along the major axis of the site from the high altar out of the front door. The energy leys usually cross over a dome of water. This is the main power center of the site.

As we discussed in Chapter Two, the Baltic coastlines of Finland and Sweden have more labyrinths per square inch than anywhere else on Earth. There are hundreds of them. I dowsed some of them in Central Sweden and on the island of Gotland, out in the Baltic. With one exception, which was probably constructed in about 1910, all of them have domes that run concurrently under one of the walls of the labyrinth, one of the veins exits out of the mouth, and the others

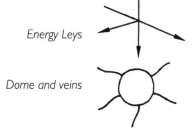

Energy Leys

Dome and veins

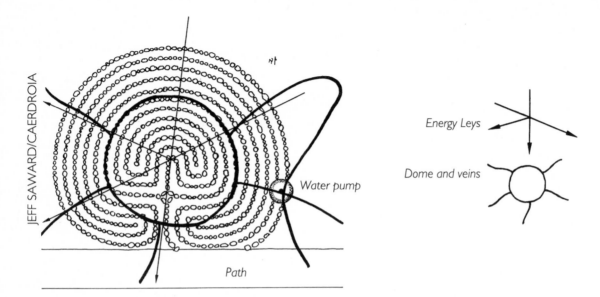

JEFF SAWARD/CAERDROIA

Energy Leys

Dome and veins

Water pump

Path

40. The Earth Energies at Fröjels Kyrka labyrinth, Fröjels, Gotland, Sweden

seem to exit at points where energy leys also enter or exit. It is the same pattern I've dowsed in many sacred places all over the Earth.

Dowsing

By now, if you are not a dowser, you must be thinking, "How does he see/dowse this energy? Am I expected to take his word for it?"

Certainly not. You can learn to see it for yourself. Dowsing, the ability to find things through the use of intuition, is a skill we seem to have devalued and lost in the last several thousand years—but, of course, it still works, and what is more, almost anyone can do it.

While there are several different dowsing tools,

for the purposes of this exercise, we will use just one: L-rods. If you are already a dowser, and you would use different tools to do these kinds of things, by all means, use the one that works most easily for you.

While store-bought L-rods are usually made out of brazing rod, most dowsers make their first pair of L-rods out of two all-wire coat hangers. With a pair of wire cutters, make one cut at one of the base wires of the C-shaped hanger itself. Make another cut at the far corner (see fig. 41). Take the longer piece of the coat hanger, and bend the angle in between to 90° degrees and, with your pliers, turn the last inch of wire at both ends 180° degrees. (This makes it safer for your eyes.) Make another L-rod just like it, and *voilà!* you have a perfectly serviceable pair of L-rods. Some like to put sleeves (wide plastic straws or copper/plastic tubing) on the shorter end of the "L". This makes it swivel more easily. The instructions will assume that your L-rods do not have sleeves.

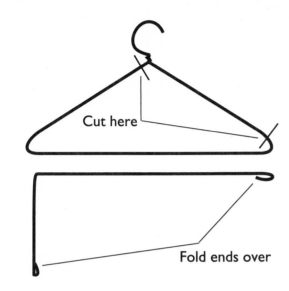

Cut here

Fold ends over

41a. Making L-rods from a wire coat-hanger

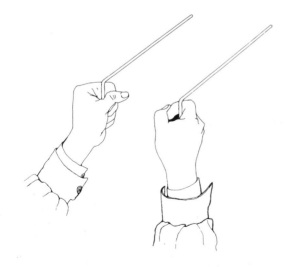

41b. L-rods in the search position

Please make yourself a pair of L-rods now. Also, find a piece of yarn or thick thread that is ten feet long or so. Put it on the floor in a straight line, perpendicular to the direction in which you are standing, three or four feet in front of you.

Hold the L-rods, fingers surrounding loosely the shorter ends of the "L". I usually rest the 90° degree turn on the pad of the second joint of my pointer/first finger(s), and hook the shorter "L" with the pad of the first joint of my pinky/little finger(s). This makes a good swivel for the L-rod to turn on. Point the rods forward, elbows somewhat bent like those cowboys with two pistols. This is called the *search position*.

Notice that as you cock your wrist upward, you will reach a point where the rods will go out or in. This is too high up. The most sensitive place to begin is to lower the tips of the L-rod just down from that point. Most dowsers hold them even lower than that, with the tips even a bit below horizontal. This is also necessary in the wind—otherwise they will swing rather wildly.

With your rods in the search position, say to yourself, "When I walk over the yarn, I want you to go out." As you approach the yarn, notice how the tips of the rods seem to feel the edge of the yarn, and begin to go/be pushed outward. When your hands are directly over the line of yarn, the rods should be out all the way, in line with the line of yarn.

Please try this now.

OK. So it might not have worked the first time. Dowsing is rather like the exercises you have been

RICHARD ELEN

doing in this book so far with the drawing of the Classical Seven Circuit Labyrinth. You began by having to think about just what point or line needs to be connected to what, but, by now, I trust that something else has happened. Your hand just seems to *gnow* where to go. Dowsing plugs in to that same kind of gnowing. When it is working, the rods seem to work by themselves. They gnow what to do.

But if they don't do that, you have to give them a little help. First of all, don't treat these dowsing tools gingerly. Don't walk tentatively towards the yarn. Do it purposefully. Move with the expectation that the tools will respond because they are working for you. Try it again.

OK. For some, the rods still may not go out. (A friend of mine has called points like this 'mind over matter'—"I don't mind, and you don't matter.") But seriously, it is your intent that the rods go out that matters, so try it again, only this time, when your hands get to the yarn line, twist your wrists outward to consciously force the rods to go outward. Do this several times to show the rods what you want them to do. Then try it again keeping your wrists steady and not twisting them outward. Usually this does the trick. If it still doesn't work, repeat this exercise several times each day for the next week or so. This repeated exercise of the intent will help your latent intuitive talents break through a lifetime of reinforcement that this kind of stuff doesn't work. We've been taught/brainwashed very well.

The Circle

Once you've felt the dowsing reaction, let's do some exercises that will help you locate and delineate these domes and energy leys. Make the line of yarn on the floor into a big circle. Stand somewhere outside the circle. Much of the time when dowsers use L-rods, they use two of them, but for the next few exercises, you will only use one of them. Hold it in either hand—whichever one feels more comfortable—out in the search position. Say to yourself, "Where's the circle? Point to the circle." Start to turn around. When the rod is pointing in the direction of the circle, you will notice that the tip seems to stick in that direction—no matter which way you turn. If that circle of yarn had been a dome at a power center, you could use this technique to find out exactly where it was.

Follow your L-rod towards the circle of yarn. Notice that as you reach the outer perimeter of the circle, the tip of the rod is pushed to one side or the other, and as you step inside the circle, the tip actually points backward—almost as if it were trying to get back to that circle. Let's first look at the inside of the circle.

Turn around and go to the inner edge of the circle. Notice that the tip of your rod goes to one side or the other (it doesn't matter which way). Move your body towards the tip of the rod. Feel it sticking to, or even pushing against that circle. Follow it all the way around.

You now can "see" where the dome is; you know both its rough circumference and diameter. Step outside the circle of yarn and face the center. Now let's look at the outer circumference of the circle of yarn. It works exactly as a mirror to the interior. Instead of having the tip pushed towards the center, it is pulled. Feel the difference. If this circle of yarn had been a dome, every time you came to an exiting vein of water, your rod would have gone quickly out, and then, just as quickly, back in. Note where these swings are, and when you come to where you began, you will

know how many veins there are. All the domes I've dowsed have an odd number of veins. Other dowsers also find this. I don't know why this is so.

Using the tip of your rod, you can then go to any one of the veins and track its course for as far as you like.

Dowsing at a Sacred Site

Where is the nearest power center to you? You gnow where it is. Maybe you've already had a picture in your mind. Maybe there's a standing stone, or a perched rock. Maybe it's a mound or some place sacred to native people. You gnow...

The most important thing to bring to such a place is respect. I also urge you to bring something else—as a gift to the place. I use tobacco. It could be a small stone that has some meaning to you, or a coin. Just a small gift to thank the place for what it will teach you.

As you did with the circle of yarn, now ask, "Please show me the closest power center with a dome." Smaller centers have a crossing of veins or even a single vein. Follow your rod to the center, and track the dome and the veins.

Dowsing Energy Leys

If you want to "see" the energy leys, you need to use both L-rods. Go out about twenty or thirty feet from the power center, and walk around the dome with your rods in the search position. Like a mantra, say over and over, "Energy leys, energy leys." This helps you focus. Assuming that there are energy leys there, as you come to the edge of one, your rods will both go out. About six to eight feet further on, they'll come back into the search position. Count how many times that happens as you walk around the circle, and divide by two (you've dowsed each energy ley twice as you walked around). Usually I find one or two energy leys—very rarely up to five. Also, you might find that when you have divided by two, you end up with, say, two-and-a-half. Energy leys have points of beginnings and endings. The "half" of an energy ley is one of these. Notice where the various energy leys run.

When you're ready to leave, remember to give thanks to the spirit of the place for teaching you.

Dowsing Labyrinths

As the largest collection of labyrinths in the world are on the Scandinavian coast, this is a good place to go to see the connection—if any—between them and the Earth energies. Just like other sacred sites on power centers, there is usually a dome and several energy leys. The most interesting thing is that the edge of the dome often runs directly under one of the walls of the labyrinth. In labyrinths with two "L's" in each quarter (the most frequent type that I saw), the dome was under the wall between paths five and six.

Each of the domes I dowsed at labyrinths of this size (eleven paths) had five veins exiting. One always went out of the path at the mouth of the labyrinth, and the others usually exited under in-coming or out-going energy leys. As far as I have seen so far, ancient labyrinths conform, as far as the Earth Energies are concerned, to the same patterns as any other pre-Protestant Reformation sacred site.

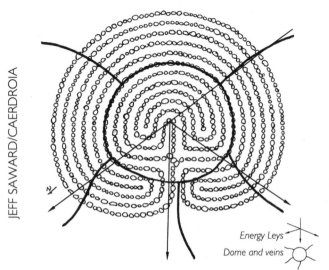

JEFF SAWARD/CAERDROIA

SIG LONEGREN

Energy Leys
Dome and veins

42. Galgberget Labyrinth, Visby, Gotland, Sweden

The Layout
—the Dome and Energy Leys

This is basically what I found at almost every labyrinth I dowsed in Sweden. From Classical Seven Circuit Labyrinths like the one at Lindbacke in Nyköping, South of Stockholm, and Galgberget and Fröjels Kyrka (both Classical Eleven Circuit Labyrinths on Gotland), to the massive Classical Fifteen Circuit Labyrinth (three "L's") at Tibble, (part of a magnificent complex of vesica-shaped stone rings, rune stones and stone rows) and Anundshög—all the older Swedish labyrinths have a dome with its outer rim running congruently with one of the walls, and the veins exiting out of the mouth and at the points where the energy leys enter or exit the labyrinth.

This is true for all the Swedish labyrinths that I visited, but one. In the village of Othem, towards the North-Eastern corner of the island of Gotland, I visited a Classical Eleven Circuit Labyrinth that a school teacher, Anton Edvard Jacobsen, had built with his class as an exercise in how their ancestors had made all the other labyrinths found on Gotland. He built it sometime in the first quarter of this century. It was an academic exercise. While the outline of the walls was clearly visible, it didn't feel right. Judging from the number of relatively large weeds growing in the path, not many people had walked it recently. Most of the others had well beaten paths. When I dowsed it, there was no dome. There were no energy leys. Just two scraggly veins crossing at random showed me that Anton Edvard was not aware of the energies when he made this one. It will work, but not as well. Dowsing can tell you interesting things about labyrinths.

A Yorkshire Turf Maze

It was early on a cold rainy morning as we left the city of York to go see my first real turf maze with Jeff and Deb Saward, editors of *Caerdroia*—the best magazine on labyrinths in the English language (if not the world). This one, outside the little village of Brandsby, is called "The City of Troy", and is found on the side of a small country road near the village.

As we stopped the car, the rain seemed to intensify, but one doesn't often get chances like this, so I jumped out and quickly surveyed the turf maze. As its name implies, the paths are made out of turf, with narrower dirt walls. It is a Classical Seven Circuit Labyrinth in form, and this one was about thirty feet across, walled in by a low white wooden fence. I decided to run it, and took off my raincoat so I could move more freely. It was exhilarating—running usually is—but surprisingly, I didn't feel any kind of spiritual presence.

43. Sig running the City of Troy Turf Maze, near Brandsby, Yorkshire, England

Disappointed and somewhat puzzled, I went back to the car to get my raincoat and my dowsing gear. When I went back to the labyrinth/turf maze, I could find no Earth energies there. Now I was totally confused. Where was the nearest power center? My rods led me down the road about thirty yards. As I turned to look back at the turf maze, I saw Jeff Saward coming up to me.

"The maze used to be where you're standing," he told me. "Some time *circa* 1900, they had a particularly wet summer. As there was an unusually muddy spot on the road in front of the maze, the farmers just pulled off the road at that point, and ran over the maze. The wheels tore it all to pieces.

"Later, some other people rebuilt the maze based on a carving of the original on a near-by barn door, but they put it down there instead." That's why there weren't any Earth Energies there. They had rebuilt it in the wrong place!

In this chapter, we have looked at two of the Earth energies many dowsers find at ancient sacred sites: domes, or blind springs, and energy leys. These energies come together, like the two poles of a battery, to create a kind of union that enhances the experiences of those on the spiritual path. There are many other Earth energies to be found at places like these. The geometry of the site enhances these energies further, and the archaeoastronomical alignments tell when the energies will be at their peak.

Dowsing is one way of looking at these energies. There are several different tools one can use to dowse, but we have concentrated on the L-rod. By now, if you have done the exercises, you can find the direction to the nearest power center, and define the dome and veins, and the energy leys that cross there. The important thing to get is the feel. How does your hand feel as the rod begins to turn? Get that feeling, and you don't need the rod.

If you are already a dowser, and have worked at sacred sites, and you don't find what I do, don't worry about it. What you are finding out for yourself is more important anyway. If you are new at this ancient art, try to find what I have dowsed, but if you find something different, and you find it consistently at sacred sites, go with what you are finding. (If you are interested in going deeper into these energies, and how to tune in to them, you might want to look at several of my other books, or the ones by Tom Graves. All are listed in the Bibliography at the back of this book.)

Lessons in Gnowing

The last half of this chapter has been a lesson in gnowing. Dowsing is a very fine tool to enhance your intuitive faculties, and if you have been successful so far, I urge you to find ways of using dowsing more and more in your life.

Another way you can use the L-rods is as a "yes" or "no" question answering device. Hold your rods in the search position. For the "no" response, your arms will go in until the arms cross. "Yes" is open. Both arms will go outward from the search position.

Try it now. Hold the rods in the search position, directly out in front of you. Say, "Show me 'no'." Expect to see the rods cross in. If they don't cross, twist your wrists slightly inward and make them do it, and say, "This is 'no'." This is the same technique you

may have used if your L-rods didn't react to the line of yarn—make them do it. Show the rods how you expect them to react.

Do the same for "yes". "Show me 'yes'." Watch the arms go out. Again, make them move correctly a few times if they don't seem to do it by themselves.

The idea is to get to a point where you are sure that you are in no way consciously moving those rods. They seem to be working by themselves. You may have to make them move for a week or more, but, with persistence, some morning you'll wake up and find that the rods seem to be working by themselves. You are then ready to use them to find the answers to "yes or no" questions. Theoretically, you can find out the answer to anything. Did you ever play "twenty questions" as a child? You have twenty questions, answerable only by "yes" or "no", to find out what your friend is thinking of.

Let's use an example. Let's say that you have lost your wallet. Obviously, there is an important need for you to find it. Take out your L-rods and say, "I need to find my wallet." While this isn't a question, notice your rods going from search position to "yes". Go back to the search position between each question.

"Is it in this house?"—yes
"Is it downstairs"—no
"Is it upstairs?"—yes
"Is it in my bedroom?"—no
"Is it in the bathroom?"—yes

At this point, it would probably pay to go to the bathroom, and let the rod show you where your wallet is. "Point to where my wallet is." Turn slowly around, and notice the direction where the rod seems to stick. Walk in that direction with both rods in the search position. Where they cross, look down. It is amazing how often it works just like that. The real and

urgent need to find what you are looking for seems to be an important factor here.

The Walls Of the Labyrinth

By now, you must be getting quite proficient at drawing the Classical Seven Circuit Labyrinth. Have you felt that click that tells you that you *gnow* how to draw one yet?

For this exercise you'll need a pencil and two different colored pens. Please start by making the basic building block of the Classical Seven Circuit Labyrinth. Do you remember how it is structured? Can you see it in your mind's eye? If not, turn to the end of Chapter Four, Figure 27 page 53, to see what it looks like. In pencil, lightly draw the basic building block towards the bottom of the center of this blank space:

Now lightly draw the walls of a left-handed (up and to the right) Classical Seven Circuit Labyrinth.

Take one of your pens and start at any one of the four "dots" that you made when you constructed the basic building blocks, and follow it to where it ends. With your other colored pen, start at either of the other dots and follow it to the end.

The walls of this Classical Seven Circuit Labyrinth are made of just two intertwining lines that cross at only one point! Spend some time looking at these two lines, and see if you can come up with some other observations on your own. Take some time and just play with it. Enjoy...

44. Blank space for drawing a labyrinth "from scratch"

CHAPTER SEVEN

THE PLANET
Mercury/Hermes—Messenger of the God/dess

WHEN ARIADNE ESCAPED from Crete with Theseus and his thirteen other Greek friends, they first landed on the island of Delos. To celebrate their liberation from certain death at the hands of the Minotaur, Ariadne led them in the Crane Dance. In this dance, everyone holds hands in a long chain, and basically follows the path of the Classical Seven Circuit Labyrinth. This back and forth pattern also mimics the mating dance of the crane—hence its name.

The Crane Dance

The crane was a bird that has been sacred to the people of the Eastern Mediterranean since pre-history. At Val Camonica in Northern Italy for example, there are rock carvings that have been dated tentatively to somewhere between 1300 and 1800 BC (see frontispiece). There is, to my knowledge, only one older petroglyph of a Classical Seven Circuit Labyrinth. It is at Luzzanas in Sardinia and could be as early as 2500 BC. The Val Camonica rock carvings also have a crane in close proximity to the labyrinth. The crane was a bird that was sacred to Mercury (Hermes in Greece), the messenger of the god/desses.

Because of the Crane Dance, which is still done on the island of Delos today, I was curious to know if there was any possibility of a connection between the planet Mercury, and the Classical Seven Circuit Labyrinth. I spoke with Mark Breen, a professional meteorologist, and curator of the planetarium at the Fairbanks Museum in St. Johnsbury, Vermont. At first, when he plotted Mercury's apparent trips back and forth around the Sun on a circular graph, it looked quite similar to the Classical Seven Circuit Labyrinth. There seemed to be some connection here, but I wasn't exactly sure what it was.

One of the ways that I tried to look at the gyrations of this innermost planet was to look at an astrological ephemeris to see if it could tell me anything. Keep in mind in the following discussion that all the astronomy I'll be talking about is naked-eye astronomy. The Greeks—and even more to the point, the pre-Hellenic peoples of the Mediterranean—didn't have telescopes. In Europe, the earliest telescopes were not in use until the beginning of the 17th century A.D., so the inventors of the labyrinth did not have them as aids for their exploration of the heavens.

In the Northern hemisphere, if you are facing the South, and look at any planet in the sky at the same time night after night, you will notice that it usually seems to be moving against the apparent clockwise (East to West) rotation of the fixed stars; however, over a longer period of time, if you were to look at the same planet each night at the same time, it would appear to be moving clockwise (West to East) in relation to the fixed stars. This normal/usual clockwise direction of any planet is referred to as going "direct". Occasionally, however, all planets, at one time or another (when they come in a direct line between the Earth and the Sun), seem to stop, and then go in the opposite direction (counterclockwise) for a while. This is called going "retrograde". They then stop (become stationary) again, and then go direct.

I noticed that in astrological terms, Mercury in most years goes retrograde three times each year, and consequently goes direct four times. This follows exactly the path of a left-handed Classical Seven Circuit Labyrinth! It goes clockwise (direct) four times, and counter-clockwise (retrograde) three.

Direct/Retrograde Motion of Mercury In One Yearly Cycle

Mercury's Directions 1991—2000

Date (mm/dd/yy)	Mercury Goes:	# of Days	Astrological Sign
1/3/91	D	91	
4/4/91	R	24	Aries
4/28/91	D	101	
8/7/91	R	24	Virgo
8/31/91	D	89	
11/28/91	R	20	Sagittarius
12/18/91	D	90	
3/17/92	R	23	Aries
4/9/92	D	102	
7/20/92	R	24	Leo
8/13/92	D	90	
11/11/92	R	21	Sagittarius\Scorpio
12/2/92	D	87	

BEGINNING OF SEVEN YEAR CYCLE

Date	Mercury Goes	# of Days	Astrological Sign
2/27/93	R	23	Pisces
3/22/93	D	102	
7/2/93	R	23	Cancer
7/25/93	D	92	
10/25/93	R	21	Scorpio
11/15/93	D	88	
2/11/94	R	22	Pisces\Aquarius
3/5/94	D	99	
6/12/94	R	24	Cancer\Gemini
7/6/94	D	95	
10/9/94	R	21	Scorpio\Libra
10/30/94	D	88	
1/26/95	R	21	Aquarius
2/16/95	D	97	
5/24/95	R	24	Gemini
6/17/95	D	97	
9/22/95	R	22	Libra
10/14/95	D	87	
1/9/96	R	21	Aquarius
1/30/96	D	94	
5/3/96	R	24	Taurus
5/27/96	D	100	
9/4/96	R	22	Libra
9/26/96	D	88	
12/23/96	R	20	Capricorn

1/12/97	D	93	
4/15/97	R	23	Taurus
5/8/97	D	101	
8/17/97	R	24	Virgo
9/10/97	D	88	
12/7/97	R	20	Capricorn\Sagittarius
12/27/97	D	90	
3/27/98	R	24	Aries
4/20/98	D	102	
7/31/98	R	23	Leo
8/23/98	D	91	
12/2/98	R	20	Sagittarius
12/11/98	D	89	
3/10/99	R	23	Aries\Pisces
4/2/99	D	101	
7/12/99	R	25	Leo\Cancer
8/6/99	D	91	
11/5/99	R	20	Sagittarius\Scorpio
11/25/99	D	88	

END OF SEVEN YEAR CYCLE

2/21/2000	R	22	Pisces
3/14/00	D	101	
6/23/00	R	24	Cancer
7/17/00	D	93	
10/18/00	R	24	Scorpio\Libra
11/10/00	D	into the year 2001…	

(Michelsen 1983)

Mercury and Astrology

In Roman mythology, Mercury was the messenger of the Gods. In his earlier Greek manifestation, he was called Hermes, and he was the cleverest of the Olympian gods. In his role of messenger, he appears in more myths than any other of the god/desses—with the possible exception of Zeus. He ruled wealth and good fortune, was the patron of commerce and thievery, and guided men on journeys. He also, like the Egyptian Anubis before him, conducted souls to the netherworld. (Can you feel his connections with the labyrinth here? It is also interesting to note that King Minos ended up as a pagan St. Peter who sat at the entrance of Hades, and judged souls. As such Minos and Mercury/Hermes would have come into frequent contact with each other.)

On the astrological level, Palden Jenkins, founder of the Oak Dragon Camps, is one of the leading-edge astrologers in Britain. (Oak Dragon offers nine-day outdoor holistic education camps on many different topics including Spiritual Traditions, Ancient Britain, Earth Mysteries, Arts and Crafts, Healing, Music and Dance, and many others.) Palden writes:

When Mercury is active, things get zappy, and there is much to-ing and fro-ing, chatter, brain rattling, tickertape, and nervous energy. Mercury activates our minds, in their capacity to receive, store, and process life-information and ideas, and in their communicative capacity. Lungs, speech organs, hands and eyes are involved too, as well as the stomach. Language, rationalizations, travel, all media of communication, and wind are all transmitters of Mercury energy. So is this book. Our nervous systems and intelligence are activated by Mercury. Mercury splits things, people, places and thoughts into separate entities, and then interrelates them by creating linkages. Observe your active mind, the flight of birds, the road traffic and people's propensity for interchange while Mercury is active. (Jenkins, *Living in Time.* 1987, p.68)

So Mercury has to do with messages and messengers—with communication. As we will see later, when we come to modern uses of the labyrinth, this is a device where one can truly get messages from the gods—answers to dilemmas that don't seem to yield themselves to rational, logical approaches.

When a planet goes retrograde, there is a relaxation of energy. Our actions seem to become nullified and undermined, and it is time to re-examine the issues at hand. Using the above charts, take a look at your own life the next time Mercury goes retrograde. Notice the increase in mis-communications between you and your friends. These are not very good times to have important talks, or to tell others of important new ideas. Fortunately, Mercury only goes retrograde three times a year, and for roughly three weeks at a time.

The Visibility of Mercury Throughout the Year

I need to digress for a moment to tell you about a slightly different maze I call Barbara's labyrinth, after the woman, Barbara Davies, who first introduced me

to it at an Oak Dragon Camp in Glastonbury. Classical Seven Circuit Labyrinths have been a part of these camps for many years. We have danced in them, used them as meditation tools, problem solving devices, and even married a couple in one! At one camp where I was leading a group that wanted to make a labyrinth in a farmer's field, Barbara shared with us a mirror of the usual Classical Seven Circuit Labyrinth that has several interesting twists. First, like the Nasca Classical Three Circuit Labyrinth, the line represents the path—not the walls. You walk on the line not between them. As such, it is a mirror of the usual one. Another similarity with the Nasca Labyrinth is that you walk the normal path in to the center, but then, instead of walking out the same way, you can cut directly out from the center to the mouth without having to retrace any of the paths. There is one of these in Hanover, Germany, called the Rad Turf Labyrinth that has a fully-grown lime tree in the center.

JEFF SAWARD/CAERDROIA

45a. Barbara's Labyrinth

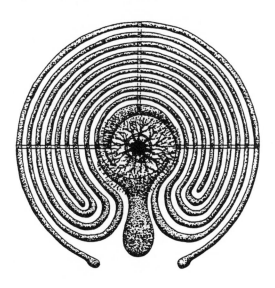

45b. Rad Turf Labyrinth, Hanover, Germany

Mercury and Venus are called interior planets because they are between the Earth and the Sun. Mercury is the closest planet to the center of our Solar system, and it never gets more than 27° degrees away from the Sun. (If you hold your hand out at arms length with your fingers parallel to the horizon, that's less than $1\frac{1}{2}$ hand-lengths: one and a half times the distance between your fingertips and your wrist. Venus gets as far away as 47° degrees from the Sun—about 3 hand-lengths.) Because of Mercury's close proximity to our major source of light and life, it can only be seen *just* after Sunset, or just before Sunrise.

As it travels in such a tight circle around the Sun, Mercury is relatively difficult to see, but there are several occasions when it is possible to catch it—again, just after Sunset or just before Sunrise depending on whether Mercury is trailing the Sun (Sunset), or leading it (Sunrise). When it is directly in front of the Sun (a conjunction, astrologically speaking, an inferior conjunction astronomically speaking—this would be analogous to the new Moon), it is invisible because the light of the Sun blocks it out. However, just before and just after its inferior conjunction with the Sun, Mercury is quite bright and therefore visible. This is not as true for its superior conjunction (when it is behind the Sun, analogous to the full Moon) as it is much farther away from us here on Earth, so its brightness is diminished. Another point when it is especially visible is when it is a great distance to one side or the other from the Sun (analogous to the half Moon.)

The Classical Seven Circuit Labyrinth represents the path the planet Mercury takes through the heavens in roughly one year as viewed from the Earth. This has to do with a marriage of two factors: the distance it travels from the Sun, and its brightness. For the purposes of this exercise, ☼ will represent Mercury at its brightest or greatest magnitude. At this magnitude, you should be able to see Mercury relatively easily. ○ will represent a medium brightness—you might be able to see it, but probably not. At ●, Mercury reflects very little light, and it is almost impossible to see.

As we have pointed out above, Mercury goes retrograde three times a year, and direct four. Mercury's year isn't the same as ours. It takes only 116 of our days for Mercury to go around the Sun. (116 x 3.15 = 365) Even so, in any given Earth Year, the pattern is roughly the same. Mercury rectifies (repeats) itself roughly every seven years. Let's use the mirror, Barbara's labyrinth, to watch Mercury's travel throughout one relatively typical year. (It will most closely follow this pattern in the years 1989, 1996 and 2003, but it is quite close in the other years as well, therefore, the description tries to cover what you might encounter during the entire seven year cycle.)

The line that bisects the labyrinth is the line between us here on Earth, and the Sun. Imagine yourself standing at the mouth of the labyrinth, and that you are looking at the Sun which is at the other end of the line. When Mercury is to the left of this line it is trailing the Sun, and therefore an evening "star". When it is to the right of the line, it is leading the Sun and therefore, a morning "star". In most years, you will see Mercury better and more often, as an evening "star"(i.e. just after Sunset).

General Rule: You'll see Mercury in most years better, and more often, in the evening than in the morning.
Visibility:
☼ high degree of brightness
○ medium degree of brightness
● low degree of brightness

1. First Path—Morning "star", January ○. As a general rule, Mercury starts out the year as a morning "star", in this case, identified by the solid black line. At this time, Mercury has medium visibility.

This particular path is called an incomplete loop as it does not double back on itself as other paths will again and again throughout the rest of the year. The final incomplete loop (eighth path) comes out from the center to join up with the solid black line to begin the next year. This is the other end of that incomplete loop that began the end of the year. For this reason, its duration as a morning star this time, is relatively brief.

2. Second Path—evening, February/March ○. This is Mercury's first appearance as an evening "star". It is difficult to see during this loop.

3. Third Path—morning, if in February ☼, in March ○, in April ○ to ●. This is the best time to see Mercury as a morning "star". It is at its maximum distance from the Sun as a morning "star" on this loop.

4. Fourth Path—evening, late spring/early summer, if in May ○, in June ○ to ☼, in July ☼. This is the best time to see Mercury as an evening "star". It is at its maximum distance from the Sun on this loop.

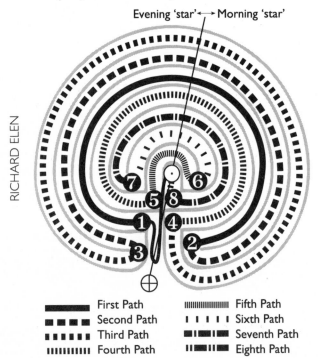

Evening 'star' ←—→ Morning 'star'

RICHARD ELEN

▬▬▬▬	First Path	‖‖‖‖‖‖‖	Fifth Path
▬ ▬ ▬ ▬	Second Path	❙ ❙ ❙ ❙ ❙	Sixth Path
▪▪▪▪▪▪	Third Path	▬❙▬❙▬	Seventh Path
‖‖‖‖‖‖	Fourth Path	❙▬❙❙▬	Eighth Path

46. Mercury's Yearly Cycle Through the Heavens

5. Fifth Path—morning, mid-summer, July and August ○.

6. Sixth Path—evening, late summer, early fall, if in September ○ to ●, in October ●, in November ● or worse. This is one of the worst times to try to see Mercury in the year.

7. Seventh Path—morning, if in November ●, in December ○. This loop occurs during Mercury's closest pass to the Sun.

8. Eighth Path—evening, late in the year, November and December ●. This is a partial loop that connects up with the solid black line/loop that begins the year.

Now, how could the ancients use this knowledge? Let's review its points of best visibility. Mercury is best seen at two very different times in its cycle through the sky. Its absolute best point of visibility either as a morning or evening "star" is when it is as far away as possible from the Sun (27° degrees on either side of the Sun) and it is going direct. It is also quite visible, *just* before Sunrise (because it is much closer to the Sun) roughly 15 days before it goes retrograde, and likewise 15 days after it goes direct, as an evening star, again, *just* before Sunset. The mid-point between these two times is called the inferior conjunction with the Sun, and Mercury can not be seen as the Sun's light blocks it out. This phase would be analogous to the new Moon, so you couldn't see it anyway.

All of this seems to be evidence that the Minoans knew quite a bit about the planet we call Mercury. As Mark Breen said, "If you were going to design something to assist you in deciding when are the best times to see the planet Mercury, the labyrinth is a good design."

When the ancients saw Mercury 1½ hand lengths (27°) away from the Sun rise or set, it was going direct. It was a very good time to use the labyrinth as a tool for predicting the future, and as a problem solving device. We can use it in the same way nowadays.

On the other hand, if you see Mercury as a morning "star" *very close* to the Sun, you know that in 15 days or so, it will go retrograde during its inferior conjunction, and at those times, there will be cross-ups in communication, and it is best to spend your time (for that three week time period) looking inside yourself and resolving issues that relate to your past rather than to your future. 15 days after it goes direct, you will see Mercury very close to the Sun *just after* Sunset. This is a clear sign that Mercury has gone direct, and it is again a good time to be using Mercurial energy to look into the future.

You can use the Mercury Direct/Retrograde charts for the 1990's to find these less than auspicious times for yourself in terms of your communications with others, and your ability to plan for the future.

I find this correlation between the Classical Seven Circuit Labyrinth and Mercury's cycle to be amazing. If nothing else, it points out one of the things our culture has lost by spending so much time inside. I have a great interest in the stars, and know most of the constellations, the names of a number of the brighter stars, and can usually identify the wanderers (the planets). To the best of my recollection, I have only seen Mercury

RICHARD ELEN

The Moon

37	78	29	70	21	62	13	54	5
6	38	79	30	71	22	63	14	46
47	7	39	80	31	72	23	55	15
16	48	8	40	81	32	64	24	56
57	17	49	9	41	73	33	65	25
26	58	18	50	1	42	74	34	66
67	27	59	10	51	2	43	75	35
36	68	19	60	11	52	3	44	76
77	28	69	20	61	12	53	4	45

Mercury

8	58	59	5	4	62	63	1
49	15	14	52	53	11	10	56
41	23	22	44	45	19	18	48
32	34	35	29	28	38	39	25
40	26	27	37	36	30	31	33
17	47	46	20	21	43	42	24
9	55	54	12	13	51	50	16
64	2	3	61	60	6	7	57

Venus

22	47	16	41	10	35	4
5	23	48	17	42	11	29
30	6	24	49	18	36	12
13	31	7	25	43	19	37
38	14	32	1	26	44	20
21	39	8	33	2	27	45
46	15	40	9	34	3	28

The Sun

6	32	3	34	35	1
7	11	27	28	8	30
19	14	16	15	23	24
18	20	22	21	17	13
25	29	10	9	26	12
36	5	33	4	2	31

Mars

11	24	7	20	3
4	12	25	8	16
17	5	13	21	9
10	18	1	14	22
23	6	19	2	15

Jupiter

4	14	15	1
9	7	6	12
5	11	10	8
16	2	3	13

Saturn

4	9	2
3	5	7
8	1	6

47. Seven magic squares and their traditional planetary associations (Michell 1983, p.124)

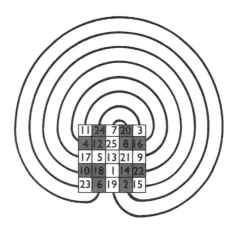

two or possibly three times in my life! Actually, under ideal conditions, the planet Mercury is visible only about fifteen to eighteen hours a year! The Classical Seven Circuit Labyrinth seems to indicate that our foremothers and fathers knew all about Mercury's movements through the sky each year, when most of us today have never even consciously seen this planet even once in our entire lifetime! And yet it *is* visible for those who have eyes to see...

Magic Squares

There is yet another connection from our esoteric heritage that links the planets with labyrinths, and this is magic squares. In John Michell's *New View Over Atlantis*, we are presented with seven orders of magic squares and their traditional planetary associations. The smallest (Saturn) consists of the numbers 1 to 9, and the largest (the Moon) has the numbers 1 to 81—arranged so that all columns, rows and diagonals add up to the same number (Saturn = 15, Jupiter = 34, Mars = 65, the Sun = 111, Venus = 175, Mercury = 260, and the Moon = 369).

One can find connections between the size of each magic square and the planet it represents. One of the more obvious is that they are arranged in order by the speed at which each planet moves in relation to the fixed stars from the slowest (Saturn) to the fastest (the Moon). It takes Saturn 29 years to go around the Sun. Each month, it barely moves at all in the sky. On average, Saturn spends roughly two-and-a-half years in each sign of the Zodiac. On the other hand, the Moon makes it around in 28+ days. It moves quite visibly in the sky night after night, and moves through each sign of the Zodiac in two-and-a-half days! The other planets and the Sun fall in between these two in exact order, according to their relative speed through the heavens as their magic squares grow in size—Saturn, Jupiter, Mars, the Sun, Venus, Mercury, and the Moon. When viewed from Earth, each one seems to move a bit faster than the planet behind it.

Please color in all of the *even* numbers in all of these magic squares, in such a way that you can still read the numbers. Please do this now.

Do you notice any interesting patterns emerging? I must admit to having been rather blown away the first time I did this. Did you see it? The magic squares with an odd number of squares on a side (Saturn, Mars, Venus and the Moon) form the basic building blocks of the Classical (Three, Seven, Eleven, and Fifteen) Circuit Labyrinths! Let's take Mars for an example:

48. The magic square of Mars with the even numbers shaded in forms the basic building block of the Classical Seven Circuit Labyrinth.

JEFF SAWARD/RICHARD ELEN

As John Michell says in his book *The New View Over Atlantis*, "The chief object for which a temple (or in this case a labyrinth) was built was to attract the gods or forces in nature to which it was dedicated.... Examples of number patterns, traditionally used for magical invocation, occur in those curious figures known as 'magic squares', in which are encodified certain numbers of reputed magical potency. Among them are the numbers found prominent in the plans of ancient temples." (Michell, 1983. p.124)

By far the most common labyrinth in the last two thousand years is the Classical Seven Circuit Labyrinth—based on the magic square of Mars. This would seem appropriate in a time of militaristic patriarchal dominance. The Hopi also relate this particular labyrinth to male energy, the Sun Father, Giver of Life. On the other hand, it is interesting to note that the labyrinth at Galgberget just north of Visby in Gotland, where the myth of the woman held prisoner comes from, is a Classical Eleven Circuit Labyrinth—based on the magic square of Venus. It is from labyrinths like this that we have developed the Goddess-in-the-center connection. Perhaps these magic squares can tell us something about the use of different Classical Labyrinths based on the number of circuits they have. But what about Mercury? Does its magic square tell us anything? As it has an even number of squares on a side (eight), it is not one of the building blocks of Classical Labyrinths.

If you spend enough time with these magical tools, you will find out all kinds of things. One of them has to do with the flow of the numbers. Each of the squares has a particular flow, and if you can discover the pattern, you can make magic squares without having to add up anything. It is a matter of following the numbers in sequential order. Let's look at the magic square of Mercury, and the first eight numbers.

Mercury

49. *The flow of the first eight numbers of the magic square of Mercury*

Now let's look at the second eight (numbers 9 to 16) and the third group of eight (17 to 24).

Mercury

RICHARD ELEN

Mercury

8	58	59	5	4	62	63	1
49	15	14	52	53	11	10	56
41	23	22	44	45	19	18	48
32	34	35	29	28	38	39	25
40	26	27	37	36	30	31	33
17	47	46	20	21	43	42	24
9	55	54	12	13	51	50	16
64	2	3	61	60	6	7	57

50. The flow of the second (previous page) and third (above) groups of eight numbers of the Magic square of Mercury

You can carry this on through all eight groups of eight numbers to complete the square, but notice how each group of eight mirrors the group behind and in front of it, and also how the same pattern contracts as you go from one series of eight numbers to the next. The flow pattern of 1 to 8 is expanded, 25 to 32 is quite contracted. Try following the series through, and see what happens. Can you find where the mirror is—where the polarity shifts?

This same pattern can be found if you turn the square on its side, and link the numbers divisible by eight (Fig. 51).

Mercury

51. The flow of the numbers divisible by eight with the magic square of Mercury turned on its side

It is identical to the flow of numbers one to eight! This thing seems to work regardless of how one looks at it. But what, if anything, does this have to do with the planet Mercury? This flow pattern is quite similar to the way the planet Mercury seems to move in relation to the Sun. Turn the square on its side, and see the flow from one to eight—Fig 52 on the next page.

RICHARD ELEN

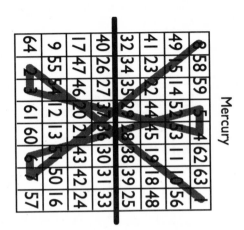

Mercury

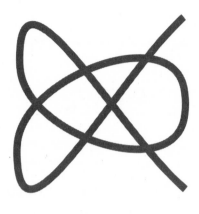

52. Mercury on its side with the flow of numbers one to eight delineated (left). A line (the mirror) is drawn down the center. Right: The flow.

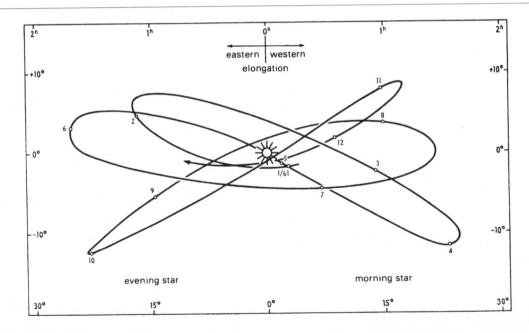

53. Mercury relative to the Sun in 1961 (From Movement and Rhythms of the Stars by Joachim Schultz. Figure 107, p.144)

Now let's look at Mercury's movement around the Sun. This information comes from an especially fine astronomy book, *Movement and Rhythms of the Stars: A Guide to Naked-eye Observations of Sun, Moon and Planets* by Joachim Schultz (Floris Books/Anthroposophic Press). As the title suggests, it shows the dance patterns of the various planets as they move through the heavens night after night, month after month, year after year. The many charts and diagrams are fantastic. One of them shows the movement of Mercury, as viewed and plotted from the Earth in the year 1961 (Fig. 53).

The line drawn down the center of the magic square in Figure 52 represents zero degrees, or the relative position of the Sun. The flows are remarkably similar.

These magic squares are truly magic. Their connection with labyrinths is clear. They can tell you much more if you're willing to put in some time "playing" with them.

Lessons in Gnowing

The labyrinth, in many ways, operates as a mirror, a reflection of something else. The right-hand labyrinth mirrors the left-handed one. And Barbara's labyrinth mirrors the Classical Seven Circuit Labyrinth in that the line becomes the path. It's like making a labyrinth in the snow. You don't make the walls and walk between them, you just walk the path. Above right is a copy of Barbara's labyrinth. Try drawing it several times—until you can do it easily:

54. Barbara's Labyrinth

So we end our discussion of Mercury talking about mirrors. Have you ever broken a thermometer and seen some liquid Mercury? Those little balls of quicksilver make excellent mirrors.

Do remember, though, that Mercury is a poisonous substance, and so is its vapor. Don't break a thermometer just to see the quicksilver, and never touch Mercury with your bare hands!

JEFF SAWARD/CAERDROIA

CHAPTER EIGHT

MIRRORS AND THE LABRYS

LABYRINTHS, IF NOTHING ELSE, are mirrors. They show us this is so in many ways. Let's take a look at the Classical Seven Circuit Labyrinth and its variant, Barbara's labyrinth, and look into the mirrors. The right-hand Classical Seven Circuit Labyrinth mirrors the left-hand one (below).

Then, Barbara's labyrinth mirrors the Classical Seven Circuit Labyrinth in that in the latter, you walk *between* the lines (the walls), whereas on the former, you walk *on* the line (the path). See Fig 56, overleaf.

These flips in polarity, these 180° turns on the labyrinth, these mirrors, are too obvious not to be noticed. And I'm sure that it comes as no surprise that one of the best metallic mirrors is Mercury—our quicksilver deity of the labyrinth (along with Ariadne and the Minotaur). Of course mercury isn't like a flat mirror. Mercury comes in little blobs—in flattened balls that reflect like a convex mirror. It's like looking through a wide angle photographic lens—it takes in more than the normal eye can, and mirrors it back to

55. Left and Right-handed Labyrinths

JEFF SAWARD/CAERDROIA

JEFF SAWARD/CAERDROIA

56. Left-handed Classical Seven Circuit Labyrinth & Barbara's mirror

you. Remember how big your nose was when you looked closely into that little blob of mercury?

The Myth and the Mirror

In the myth, Theseus went and met his mirror—the Minotaur. The beast, Theseus' shadow, was half Goddess/human, half God/animal—his grandfather was Poseidon, and his mother Pasiphaë was originally worshipped as white cow goddess of the Moon. The monster's mirror, Theseus, was of royal, but human, blood. He could at times command the gods—as he did when he called down Poseidon's wrath on his own son Hippolytus when he was married to Phaedra.

Over years of primping or combing our hair, we've forgotten that a mirror doesn't reflect back exactly how it looks: it's backwards—left becomes right—but top doesn't become bottom. Some say that is how it is on higher realms: left becomes right, time runs in a

different direction. Perhaps this is why some psychics have difficulty in telling time—telling exactly when something is going to happen. How you perceive it *there* isn't exactly how it is perceived *here*. It's switched somehow, like a mirror. We're going to spend most of this chapter looking at this switch—this mirror.

The Chakras

Dowsing can help you experience this switch of polarities between the various levels. This can be seen when you dowse the polarities of the chakras. The chakras are nodes of power, and while there are many configurations of these power points within our bodies, many schools have settled on seven primary ones running from the base of the spine to the top of the head. When you dowse them from the root chakra up, they flip in polarity as you go from one to the next one up. These flips act like mirrors.

The Labyrinth is complete!

The root chakra, at the base of the spine, vibrates at the lowest rate. It represents the physical world, Earth.

The second chakra up is found two or three fingers below the navel, and is called the splenic chakra. Among other things, it is associated with feelings, emotions and sexual issues. This is a point that is activated, among other times, at moments of deep stress. It's that pit-of-the-stomach feeling. It is also the place where we defend ourselves from the outer environment, and it is usually highly armored. It is the realm of the element Water.

The Solar chakra is found in the solar plexus, just below the center of the rib cage. The mind, memory and other kinds of mental activity focus here. This is the chakra of Fire.

The heart chakra is right over your heart, and lies in the center of these seven chakras—three are below, and three are above. At your center is your spiritual essence. The heart chakra holds your own personal spiritual bundle—"How is your spiritual life going?" The answer comes from your heart. Here is found the element Air.

The throat chakra marks the point of our voice box, the initiator of sound. It is a point of communication—but not the only one: there are heart to heart talks and second chakra points of (sexual) intercourse as well. The throat chakra is the point where things become manifest. Below the throat are the four Elements (Earth, Water, Fire and Air) that make up the physical world. Above are the higher invisible realms. Adam's first job in the Garden of Eden was to name the animals. The throat chakra is where naming takes place (Adam's Apple). When you can name something, you can control it. When you know the jargon, you have a handle on how to work it. Do you know these words—"RAM", "ROM", "DOS", "hard disk" and "backup"? If you do, you probably have worked with/ use/know how to control computers. Every occupation has its jargon. Learn it, name it, and you can manifest things in that field.

The brow chakra is the Hindu third eye that is marked with paint or gemstones on the foreheads of women from the Indian sub-continent. This point between, and just above, the eyebrows marks the screen that you dream on.

Try this Exercise:

Close your eyes and picture your best friend.... Then open your eyes.

The place where you saw them is at the brow chakra.

Each chakra going up the spine vibrates more rapidly than the one below it, and not as rapidly as the one above it. This increase in vibration culminates at the crown chakra, at the top of the head. This holds the One, the vibration that some call God, Goddess, or Great Mystery. It is Unconditional Love.

These chakras represent the entire vibratory spectrum of the cosmos, from the lowest vibratory level—the physical plane, down at the root chakra—to the most rapid One at the crown chakra.

(Important note: if you are already familiar with the chakras, and have a different concept of what each chakra means, by all means, use your system rather than mine! This is the Gnostic way. The forms change, but the circle of Light remains.)

Try this Exercise:

Find a friend who is willing to have their chakras dowsed. Hold your L-rod in one hand, and put the pointer finger of your other hand on the top of your friend's head (on their crown chakra). If your friend is a woman, your L rod will go in, if a man, it will go out. Run your finger down the back of your friend's head. Notice how your L rod will go back into the search position (straight in front of you). When you reach the point where the third eye/brow chakra is located, your L rod will do the opposite of what it did at the crown chakra indicating a polarity switch. This flipping back and forth will continue as you run your finger down your friend's spine down to the tail bone/root chakra.

We all have some of each—yin and yang within us. Women have four yin chakras and three yang. Men mirror that; we have four yang chakras and three yin.

Name of chakra	Dowsed Polarity if female	Dowsed Polarity if male	Key Word
7. Crown	- (yin)	+ (yang)	God/dess
6. Brow	+	-	Vision
5. Throat	-	+	Manifest
4. Heart	+	-	Personal Spiritual
3. Solar	-	+	Mental
2. Splenic	+	-	Emotional/Astral
1. Root	-	+	Physical

57. Dowsing the Chakras

Mirrors

The implication here is that when one moves from one level to another (say from the physical to the astral/emotional), things flip. It's like going in to a mirror. What have we heard about working with mirrors in this way? Alice went through the Looking Glass to visit other worlds. She had to change drastically in size in order to fit into the various kingdoms she visited. Scrying—foretelling the future by looking into something reflective, like a bowl of water, a crystal ball, a mirror—is an ancient art practised by many cultures.

"It's done with mirrors." How often have you heard that said to explain some stage magician's incredible trick? Like chemists who trace their roots back to alchemists, and the doctor who has his beginnings in a particularly female occupation—a knowledge of healing herbs, midwifery, and other healing arts—the stage magician traces his roots back to a time when there were those who actually could do *real* magic—the Merlins, the true Magi. And they used mirrors as well—but not in the same way.

In Ireland there are enormous mounds with chambers—often cruciform (shaped like a cross)—inside them. Built in prehistory, at least 3,000 to 4,000 BC, these chambers are oriented towards significant horizonal astronomical events. The one at New Grange is oriented towards the Winter Solstice Sunrise. Cairn T at Loughcrew, north-east of Dublin in Ireland, is another cruciform chamber, where I witnessed the Spring Equinox Sunrise. The light of that rising Sun focused sharply on the back wall, and moved slowly from left to right across an enormous stone that formed the back wall of the chamber. The climax came when it seemed that the Sunlight was about to

eat a circle with an eight-petaled daisy inside it—both pecked into the face of that boulder in the back of the chamber. Jaws of Sunlight that were just the right size opened to engulf the circle and flower. And then, for a few brief moments, the Sun obliterated the circled daisy from view with its power. And then it moved on...

That is just one way to use the Light in a chamber like this. In many of these Irish chambered cairns, archaeologists found large flat stone bowls. Fortunately, some were so big that they could not be rolled down the tunnel and out of the mouth to some museum, so they are still there! They must have been put in there at least before the roof was put on. But what were these enormous circular bowls used for? I see them filled with holy water from a nearby sacred spring. On the day the Sun (or Moon) lines up with the mouth of the chamber, a beam of Sun or Moon light, like the male organ, enters into the womb of the Earth Mother. At the point of farthest penetration of the light lies the flat bowl with its flat surface of water—a mirror. What happened when that beam of Light hit that waiting bowl of water and stone? What kind of scrying went on at that point? I'll leave that up to your imagination, but it looks like magicians were working with mirrors at least as far back as 4,000 BC—some say 7,000 BC. I don't mean in any way to imply by the use of the word "magician" that I am excluding female workers of magic. Actually, according to Janet McCrickard, author of *Eclipse Of the Sun*, the mirror was the symbol of the Sun Goddess, and therefore used by women.

Mirrors and Fairy Tales

"Mirror mirror on the wall, who's the fairest...?" It doesn't lie. For many years, Snow White's step-mother had been a raving *femme fatale*—the fairest of them all, but she was growing older. She didn't gnow that wisdom blossoms as beauty fades. The mirror just reflects physical "reality". The mirror isn't subjective, it speaks objective truth. The spirit in the mirror won't even lie for its mistress, Snow White's wicked stepmother, not even to please her. It can't. It reflects objective reality: "truth."

In a telescope, the first lens that the light hits is called the objective lens. It focuses the light, and in the process, turns it upside-down! Doesn't it strike you as odd that these things that our society calls objective turn things upside-down or left to right? But let's follow this thread further...

If the mirror is objective reality, does that makes us, the viewer, by implication, subjective? Twylah Nitsch is a Seneca Indian Grandmother of the Haudenosaunee (Iroquois) Confederation. She is a Wolf Clan Mother, and a greatly respected teacher of her people's spiritual path. She uses the Seneca Medicine Wheel which has many different overlays. At its most simple, the Medicine Wheel is a circle with the four directions, East connected to West and South connected to North, making a cross. The Druids in Britain hold this symbol dear as well.

RICHARD ELEN

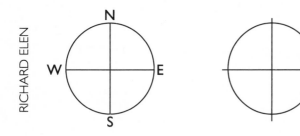

58. The Medicine Wheel and the Druid's Cross

The Circle is the wheel of life. As each one of us sits at a slightly different point on the Medicine Wheel, so each one of us sees things just a little bit differently. Each one of us has our own subjective view of reality. Twylah calls it our sacred point of view. We each have our own individual sacred point of view.

The horizontal (East/West) line represents our Earth Walk, what we are given to do while we are here walking this path. The vertical (North/South) line Twylah calls the "Pathway of Truth." It holds our Wisdom in the North, and our Faith in the South.

The point where our Earth Walk is crossed by the Pathway of Truth is called our vibral core—whether it is an individual one, a community one, or the Cosmic One. This vibral core will prove to be an important point.

I was talking with a woman named Wata, a student of Grandmother Twylah's who teaches the medicine wheel path at a local college. I had been sharing my fascination with mirrors, and Wata asked if I had seen the work of Bev Doolittle, an artist from Western Massachusetts who paints pictures where there are clearly several levels of reality going on at the same time. One of her pictures, called *Sacred Ground*, is long and quite narrow. It is a picture of the trunks of a

white birch forest in the snow. On the right-hand third of the picture is a man on a horse leading another horse riding to the right—off the picture. But what of the rest of the picture—what of the other two-thirds of the picture that was nothing but a lot of white birch tree trunks with those black triangular spots that mark where branches leave the trunk? And then I saw the eagle in the black dots—and other forms.

Wata offered me a mirror to look at the reflection of the picture. Suddenly there, in the trees, springing out of the painting were three eagles and a male Indian's profile!

These kinds of hidden pictures, or natural likenesses, are found throughout Nature—especially at power centers, and are called 'simulacra' by John Michell, who has written a book about them subtitled *Natural Likenesses—Faces and Figures In Nature*. This vision of the spirit world was easier to see through a mirror.

Wata then drew a picture of how the eye "sees" something. In this case, let's say it is a tree. The lens of the eye performs the same function as the objective lens on a telescope. The lens is at the crossing point where the switch takes place. It focuses the image, and in doing so, projects an upside-down image of the tree on the back of the eye where the rods and cones pick it up and send it to the brain where it is turned right-side up again. Wata talked of the eye side of the lens (us) as being objective, and what is out there beyond the lens as being subjective. This is the lens through which we view our Earth Walk, and it's upside down!

Wata drew this picture, and intersected the lens with a vertical line that represented the Pathway of Truth.

RICHARD ELEN

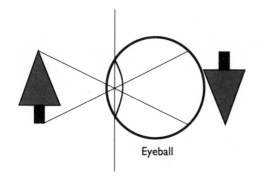

Eyeball

59. The Eye and The Pathway Of Truth

I looked at Wata's drawing, and suddenly, with that flash that comes when one sees simulacra, I wasn't looking at a representation of that eye looking through a lens that is bisected by the Pathway of Truth, I was looking at a *labrys*—the sacred double-headed axe of the Minoan Civilization, the magical scepter of the Amazons.

But in Portugal, the Goidelic Celts appropriated that ancient symbol of female power, and changed it to mean "chief", "reason", or "dog". There was a switch, a flip in polarities from female to male, from Goddess to "chief", from subjective/intuitive to "objective". (I'm not exactly sure where the "dog" fits in here—unless earlier there was a connection with cats?) Like the labyrinth myth itself, the labrys was taken over by the patriarchal Indo-Europeans. They usurped the labrys, a symbol of feminine power, and turned it into the masculine symbol of power—the "chief", or the new way of thinking—"rational". What a mirror this labrys turns out to be!

The Labrys and Sacred Geometry

The double-headed labrys is interesting from a sacred geometrical point of view. The Pythagorean theorem, $a^2 + b^2 = c^2$, is the formula for computing any side of a right angled triangle if the other two sides are known. It is one of the major contributions of this Greek teacher to modern consciousness in the world of geometry. According to Professor Alexander Thom, a currently much-attacked pioneer archaeoastronomer, geometrical designs are the heart of many of the stone rings in Britain that he surveyed. One of these designs that ends up looking remarkably like an egg, includes the use of two 3-4-5 right-angled triangles at its heart.

If you create two 3-4-5 right-angled triangles, and connect them on the 4 sides, you've created one of the blades of the labrys. By using two more 3-4-5 right-angled triangles, you can then make the other "head". I had heard over fifteen years ago that on the latitude of the Mediterranean, if you hold the handle pointing to the North Star, the "5" sides/hypotenuses point towards significant horizonal astronomical events—I thought I had heard it was connected with the Sun. It wasn't.

First of all, let's look at some simple geometry. If you took it in high school, you'll easily be able to follow this. If not, give it your best shot. A right triangle (ABC) has one right angle (90°)—in this case, the angle CAB. The other two angles (<ABC and <BCA) must add up to 90°. The interior angles of a 3-4-5 right-angled triangle are known, and can be looked up in any school geometry text book—<ABC = 53.13°. Therefore, 90° - 53.13° = <BCA, or 36.87°.

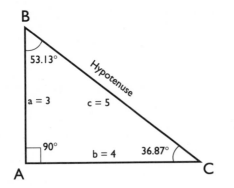

60. *a² (side BA) + b² (side AC) = c² (side BC), also called the hypotenuse.*

By aligning two similar triangles along the "4" side, you create one blade. Do the same again, and you have both blades of the double-headed axe of the Goddess, the labrys.

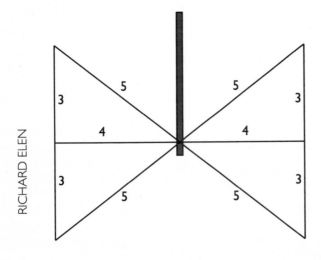

61. *3-4-5 Labrys*

Now, point the handle (Twylah's Pathway of Truth) to the North. I have a computer printout created by Anthony Aveni, an archaeoastronomer from Colgate University in Hamilton, New York, USA, who is one of the leading lights in Meso- and South American prehistoric astronomy. The print-out gives an incredible amount of information. For each degree of latitude he lists all the major Solar and Lunar horizonal events, and stellar (star) ones as well for 500-year time periods starting at 1500 AD and working back in 500-year increments, back to 1500 BC, the date I used which is roughly one-hundred years before the birth of the Minotaur, and assumes a level horizon.

The Moon

But first, some talk of the Moon. Basically, it not only mirrors the light of the Sun, but it mirrors the Sun's path as well. The full Moon rises in the Eastern sky mirroring the Sun as it sets in the West. Perhaps you've noticed that in the Summer, when the Sun is high in the sky, the Moon skirts the horizon. Conversely, in the dark winter nights of Northern climes, the Moon rides high in the Southern sky. At the same time of year, the Sun at noon rides low in the Southern sky.

I want to say this another way. On the longest day of the year, the Summer Solstice Sun rises in the *North*-East (exactly where depends on what latitude you're on). The full Moon nearest that Summer Solstice rises in the *South*-East around the point on the horizon where the Winter Solstice Sun rises, and sets in the South-West, around the point where the Winter Solstice Sun Sets.

At the Winter Solstice, it is exactly the other way around. The Sun rises in the South-East and sets in the

South-West; the nearest full Moon rises in the North-East, around the point of the Summer Solstice Sunrise and sets in the North-West, around the point of the Summer Solstice Sunset. The Moon is a mirror that does the exact opposite of the Sun.

Notice that I said the Moon rose *around* the point of, say, the Summer Solstice Sunrise. Year after year, the Full Moon nearest to the Winter Solstice does not rise at the same point on the horizon. It dances around the point of the Summer Solstice Sunrise. For about 9.3+ years, it moves to the South, until it reaches what is called the Northern Minor Standstill of the Moon. Then it turns North, when after another period of 9.3+ years, the Moon reaches the most Northerly point on the North-Eastern horizon that it ever reaches. This is called the Northern Major Standstill of the Moon, and it happens only once every 18.67 years. It is called the Metonic Cycle after the Greek who "discovered" it as a way to more accurately regulate the shorter cycles.

Likewise, there is a Southern Major Standstill of the Moon in the South-East once every 18.67 years around the time of a Summer Solstice. It rises as far South in the South-East as it ever does, and sets as far South in the South-West as it ever does.

If you don't have a Farmers' Almanac, in order to predict eclipses, it is imperative that you know about these Major and Minor Standstills of the Moon. (For example, if on the Summer Solstice, the full Moon rises exactly where the Winter Solstice Sun rises, a point exactly half way between the Southern Major and Minor Standstill points on the horizon, there will be an eclipse, as the Moon is at the point where the plane of the path of the Moon intersects the plane of the Earth. This is called a "dragon's node" by astrologers, and the "ecliptic" by astronomers.

One of the most ancient of all Europe's megalithic remains, Gavrinis, is a chambered cairn on an island just South of Carnac in Brittany, France. Its major axis is oriented to the Southern Major Standstill of the Moon. It has some of the most complex artwork pecked into the inner faces of the interior megalithic boulders that I have ever seen. Each stone looks like a great big fingerprint whorl.

This megalithic chambered cairn also picks up the Sun as well. Looking out of the mouth, if you stand in the right-hand corner of the back of the chamber, you can just catch the Winter Solstice Sunrise at the left-hand side of the mouth of the chamber.

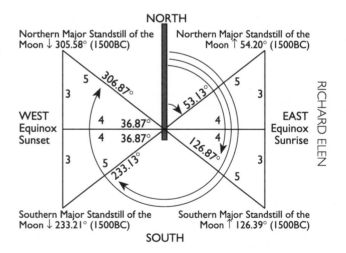

62. 3-4-5 Labrys and astronomy at the latitude of Crete (35°) in 1500 BC assuming a level horizon. The more North in latitude you go, the wider the axe head

At the latitude of Knossos, 35°, using the figures supplied by Anthony Aveni's print-out for 1500 BC, and given a level horizon, if you point the handle of the axe at the Pole Star (at the time of Theseus this was a star named "Thuban" in the constellation Draco, the Dragon), the non-cutting edge of the labrys pointing to the North-East will align with the Northern Major Standstill of the rising Moon, and the North-West edge will point to the Northern Major Standstill of the setting Moon. Conversely, the edge pointing South-East aligns with the Southern Major Standstill of the rising Moon, and to the South-West, the Southern Major Standstill of the setting Moon! This only works at the latitude of Crete (35°)!

Incidentally, as at Gavrinis, there's a Solar connection with this labrys as well. The line that Twylah would call the Earth Walk, drawn perpendicularly to the axe handle at the center of the "X" (along the "4" lines of the 3-4-5 right angled triangles), align due East West—thus marking both Equinox Sunrises and Sets! But for the Minoan Civilization, a labrys with these Pythagorean ratios would have been primarily a tool for keeping track of a very major cycle of the Moon.

Very early on, Stone Age people were aware of the Moon and its cycles. There is evidence that the Magdalenian people of 11,000 to 13,000 BC were aware of the cyclical nature of the Moon. Alexander Marshack, a Research Fellow of the Peabody Museum of Archaeology and Ethnology at Harvard University, examined a bone of an eagle found at a Magdalenian site called Placard in South-Western France. The bone had several rows of linear scratches—almost rune-like, but smaller—that he determined to be evidence of these people's awareness of what he calls "lunar phrasing". He also determined that that particular bit of Eagle's bone had been used to record precisely one lunar year!

Our species has studied the cycles of the Moon for a long long time. The labrys has its ongoing association with Goddess, and its possible use as a tool (at least in the Mediterranean) to mark all the Major Standstills of the Moon. Pasiphaë was a Goddess of the Moon, often pictured with a white cow, the horns representing the crescents of the Moon. The labrys was more than a weapon of war, it was a magical tool of power for those who walked with Goddess.

The Eye of the Labrys

What is this "objective" lens that is found in telescopes or in our own eyes, that turns the image upside down? What is that point where the Earth walk is intersected by the Pathway Of Truth? What is that mirror in the crossing of the two heads of the labrys?

Please try this experiment:

Get yourself into a sitting position. Hold your arm, pointer finger extended, above your head, and focus on the tip of that extended finger. You might find it easier to close one eye. Rotate your arm in a small circle so that you can see that your finger is going in a clockwise direction. Continue to rotate your arm but bring your finger slowly down from above your head to the area of your heart. In what direction is your finger going? Please try this now.

The Switch

It's going the other way! Like a mirror, the direction flipped. (If you don't see this the first time, try again. Some folks do have difficulty in seeing this, but when they keep at it, they finally do see it.)

As with any magic trick, the next question might be, "OK, where did the switch take place?" "Where is the eye of this labrys?"

It's in *your* eye. Go back again to where we began, and start with a clockwise rotation. Remember to keep one eye closed. Bring the spiral down slowly until the finger nail on the finger you are pointing with is level with your eyes. Continue to move your arm in the circular clockwise direction. At that point where the plane of your eye meets the plane of the finger nail, something magic happens. Your finger nail looks like it's just going back and forth. There's no depth, so you can't tell which direction your arm is rotating in!

Hold your arm up in the air one more time, only this time, make your finger go in a counterclockwise direction. Bring it down to eye level. I don't know about you, but I can't tell any difference at all between a finger that is going clockwise or counterclockwise—they both at this point look like they are simply going back and forth.

This is the switch point, the eye of the labrys.

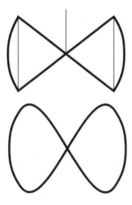

63. The Labrys and the Lemniscate (∞)

There is another symbol that looks very much like a labrys, it's called a lemniscate—∞. It's that sideways "8" that means infinity—it goes on forever. The Earth has some examples of this lemniscate. The Atlantic Ocean is a good one. Think of the Gulf Stream. It starts down in the Caribbean, where a large injection of warm water runs up the coast of the United States and Canada. It is confronted by the Labrador Current, and the Gulf Stream turns to the right, and goes over to Ireland and Britain. There are palm trees in South-Western England courtesy of the warm water from the Caribbean. While some of the Gulf Stream goes North-East to warm the coast of Norway, a portion of it turns South along the coasts of France, the Iberian peninsula and North-Western Africa, and then back across the Atlantic to the Caribbean where it begins all over again. The Gulf Stream runs in a clockwise direction.

In the Southern Atlantic, it's exactly the opposite. Cold waters from the Antarctic flow up along the west coast of Africa. Around the Gulf of Guinea, they turn westward across the Atlantic where the water is warmed. This current hits the Eastern tip of Brazil, turns southward along the coast of South America, and back down into the Antarctic Ocean. This current runs in a counterclockwise direction. These two swirling circular streams form a lemniscate (8 or ∞).

So where do these differently rotating currents meet (as do similar ones in the Pacific)? Where is the "X"? Where's the switch? Where's the mirror? It is at the Equator, where things are equal, the point of balance. These currents form a beautiful lemniscate on the surface of our planet with the "X" at the Equator. It is also found in the labrys—that eternal going in and going out, on higher levels, from the spiritual to the physical, and back to the spiritual.

The chakras demonstrate this lemniscate in many ways, but perhaps one of the best, visually, is one that crosses at the neck where the throat chakra is found. The four lower chakras in this model represent physical manifestation of the four elements:

Heart chakra= Air = personal spiritual
Solar plexus = Fire = mental
Sacral = Water = emotional
Root = Earth = physical

In the Western Mystery tradition, the fifth chakra, the throat, is equated with something called the etheric. This is where the elements go when the form changes. For example, when an ice cube (Earth) is warmed up, it turns to a liquid, water (Water). Where did the Earth element go? Occultists say it went up into the ether, and the Water element returned. Heat the water up a bit and it turns to steam—water to fire, and the same process occurs again—the Water goes back to the ether, and the Fire/steam comes down. Vaporization carries this to the final step on the physical level, up to the element of Air.

The throat is the initiator here. It makes things manifest and unmanifest. So the lower loop of the lemniscate, representing physical reality, goes from the throat, down to the root chakra, and back up to the throat, the "X", the point of manifestation. This physical loop includes four chakras. The upper loop represents the spiritual realms, and is shorter in length than the physical loop in that it goes to the crown chakra, and therefore includes only two chakras, the center of spiritual vision, and the One, the source from which everything emanates.

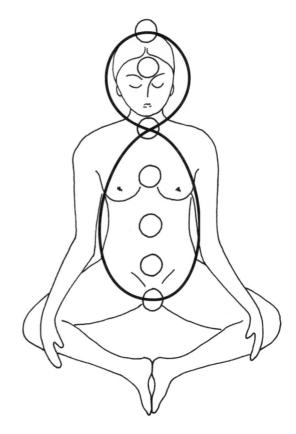

64. Lemniscate and the Chakras

The labrys is a fascinating tool on many levels, but what connections can we make between the labrys and the labyrinth, the focus of this book? Aside from their linguistic connections along with "labia", all indicating a feminine aura about them, both the labyrinth and the labrys meet up in Knossos, one of the last vestiges of the Goddess in the Mediterranean. The

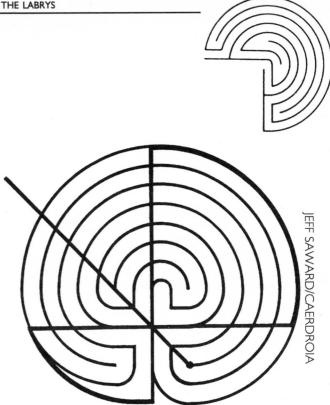

labrys was a ceremonial tool used in the sacrifices of the bulls that were so important in Minoan ceremony and myth. The labyrinth held the half-bull/half-man, the Minotaur. The labyrinth has roots with Goddess and Mercury—the labrys with the Moon.

But perhaps the most important connection is that both the labrys and the Classical Seven Circuit Labyrinth have an "X" at their heart. This node, this switch, this mirror is a point where energy, the four elements, can be transformed. It is the point where direct and individual communication with spiritual realms, the God/dess, occurs.

If I were brash enough to suggest that there might be a way of putting the labrys on a left-handed labyrinth, it would seem to me that in the lower left-hand quadrant is the mouth, which also can represent the physical. It is where we stand to view the Sun in the center, or goal. In the upper right-hand quadrant is the Sun, the goal, the spiritual. These make up the two blades of the labrys—the two extremes of the physical and the spiritual. The other two quadrants mark the middle of the labyrinth; they mark the beginning and end of the middle path (number four) of the seven paths. Astronomically speaking, these would be the two equinox points: the equator in our lemniscate of the currents of the Atlantic Ocean. A line drawn from the dot in the upper left-hand quadrant, through the center of the "X" to the dot in the lower right-hand quadrant, would represent the handle of the labrys: Twylah's Pathway of Truth.

I keep thinking about that point of the crossing of the two lines, that infinitesimally small speck —and yet we have to go so far to get to the opposite side of that speck/door from where we are starting from, here in the physical. Wouldn't it be easier to just step across the "X"? So near, and yet so far...

JEFF SAWARD/CAERDROIA

65. The Labrys on the Labyrinth

The paths of the labyrinth in this model of the labrys on the labyrinth, mark the travels of Mercury, who is madly running back and forth between the two, being the messenger and providing communication for those who have ears to hear. Mercury is the god of road crossings, where two roads meet and make an "X".

Mercury's Mirror

We've been talking a great deal about Mercury and mirrors. Does Mercury have a mirror? Just as the myth of labyrinth and the symbol of the labrys were taken over by the patriarchy to be used for their own, polarized ends, is there someone in Herstory whom Mercury supplanted? Who was Mercury's mirror?

As Mercury is the God of the crossing of four roads, Hecate is the Goddess of the three ways.

Goddess took three forms—the virgin, the mother, the wise old woman. The Christian Church only allowed one of these three forms of the Goddess to come through—the virgin.

Hecate is portrayed as an old woman. A wise old woman. Any point where three roads come together is sacred to her. She is the Goddess of the latter third of our life, the goddess of wisdom. The goddess of death. For this last reason, she is also depicted as a crone.

Both Hecate and Mercury are deities of the West, and of death. (Hermes was the evening "star" we call Mercury.) Hecate brings death, Mercury supports the soul as it makes the transition to the other world.

Hecate comes before, and brings death. Mercury/Hermes/Anubis helps you on the cusp, at the point of transition. (Isn't it an interesting reflection that some say that it is another manifestation of Mercury—as the stork/crane—that brings you in to this life?)

We live in a culture that in so many ways denies death and old age—look at the focus on being young and attractive (Snow White's Stepmother?). Hecate brings death. We don't want to look Her in the face any more than Western man wants to look at his shadow. We certainly don't seek her wisdom, and anyway, there can't be a wise old woman Goddess as an archetype in a patriarchal religion and culture. So, we got rid of her. We used ridicule. Who wants to be seen as being hecate-peckate—going here and there without purpose? It's like "meander". Mercury came in and took over the road crossings, the doors. The three became four.

"Three roads" in Latin is *tri via, tri-via,* trivia. We've trivialized Her!

CHAPTER NINE

HIS STORY

Over the past few years, I have been having a fascinating on-going correspondence with Ronald Hutton, a very knowledgeable friend to have when one wants to know how the archaeologists and prehistorians of the 1990's view British and European prehistory. He is the Reader in British History at Bristol University. I came to know Ronald at Oak Dragon where we worked together on some "Ancient Britain" camps. He represented academia's view of British prehistory. And he did it well. It is to Ronald that I owe much of my awareness of where archaeology is today.

Ronald has pointed out to me that the word 'history' comes from the Latin *historia* which means 'a true story', and it is feminine in gender (it ends with an "a"), not masculine, as I have been portraying this word throughout this book. The Romans felt that "Historia", or truth in stories, came from the Muses, from our feminine side. And yet, look at who wrote history— the victors, the men. Again and again mirrors, switches in polarity, play a part in this tale.

The Old Gods of Archaeology

I received my Masters Degree in Sacred Space in 1979. While there were very interesting deviant interpretations of British pre-history like Alfred Watkins' *The Old Straight Track*, Janet and Colin Bord's *Mysteri-* *ous Britain*, and John Michell's *View Over Atlantis*, if one wanted to know what the establishment archaeologists thought about prehistory, one would read works by Glynn Daniel, Gordon Child, Mortimer Wheeler, Stuart Piggott, and Professor R.J.C. Atkinson. These were the Greats of British Archaeology of the first two-thirds of this century. Their view of prehistory was the accepted one.

In the nineteen-sixties and seventies, as a result of revolutionary scientific techniques like the recalibration of radio carbon dating, pollen analysis, and developments in the field of the pathology of bones, there was a revolution within the archaeological community itself. Newer, more advanced data gathering was showing that the theories of the Giants in British Archaeology were not made of whole cloth. In some cases their preservation of material was totally inadequate. With others, it was their own projection of what went on in prehistory that influenced what they saw at their digs. (I suspect that this plays a role in *any* view of history— or herstory for that matter.) One of those shared projections had to do with Goddess and Her importance in pre-history.

The New Archaeologists

Today, the new breed seems to operate in a shark tank where no one dares to publish until they have joined a team of at least ten others who have chewed it all up and caught any errors. Then it's safe to publish. These new archaeologists and prehistorians would have us see a very different vision of that time before the written word than either the one held by the Grand Old Men of British Archaeology, *or* the view that those who hold Goddess dear have. Goddess-lovers see a Golden Age in European herstory where healers—skilled with the use of wild herbs and other techniques—cured the sick, when the people walked in harmony with the land, a time when all defensive perimeters around villages and towns were not necessary, but most importantly, in that time of peace, when Goddess reigned supreme.

The Golden Age Exposed

When today's archaeologists look at the bones of pre-historic Britain, they find evidence of what Gordon Child spoke of as "a short and brutish life". Most were dead before their thirtieth birthday, due to all the same kinds of things that affect us: tetanus, arthritis, polio, spina bifida, tooth abscesses and sinusitis. These neolithic people did not exactly live disease-free lives.

Living in harmony with the environment is at least questionable with our prehistoric foremothers and fathers. First of all, living in harmony does not mean living disease-free, or that people lived long lives. In Mesolithic times, they were beginning to clear the forests. By the Iron Age in Britain, large portions of the Lake District were irrevocably changed from woodland to bog. Dartmoor in Devon, once covered with oak and other hardwoods, is now mostly bracken (ferns), heather and low grasses that the sheep and Dartmoor ponies survive on. The moor rolls on for miles with hardly anything growing above one's knees, except for the recent pine plantations, and the very rare tastes—like Wistman's Wood—of what Dartmoor used to be before Bronze and Iron Age people cut most of the trees down. The Brazilian rain forest 'cut-it-down' mentality is not new. It happened on Dartmoor and in the Lake District in the second millennium before Jesus. The environmental impact is clear to see, three thousand years later. This is not the sentimental nostalgic view of native peoples walking lightly on the land. Unfortunately, our prehistoric forefathers were equally capable of raping the land.

Defensive Walls

Now for the defensive walls issue. Çatal Hüyük in Anatolia, Turkey, one of the Heartlands of the feminist Goddess visions, has defensive walls. While it is true that Knossos, the capital city of the Minoan Empire, did not have defensive walls around it, it is important to remember that Minos had his navy, and it was the best in that area of the Mediterranean at that time. (Some even say it was the world's first.) Living on an island, Minos didn't need defensive positions against his own people, and his indomitable navy took care of everyone else. Minoan trading outposts of that time in other lands were fortified.

In Britain, many have assumed that the Iron Age hill forts were the first real defensive positions on that island. Recent archaeological evidence has shown, however, that Crickley Hill in Gloucestershire was heavily fortified in 3200 BC. And even further back, at Carn Brea in Cornwall, Dr Robert Mercer showed

that the people there had constructed a massive stone wall in 3800 BC.

By the fifth millennium BC, in the heartland of Marija Gimbutas' Old Europe, towns like Polyanitsa in Bulgaria, were acquiring town walls. Defensive positions go way back.

The Indo-Europeans

Another challenge that modern historians throw at herstorians and the Grand Old Men alike is, "Please stop calling them the Indo-Europeans. There can't possibly have been one group/culture/race that covered such a long space of time." The Proto-Indo-European *Kurgans* of Marija Gimbutas came into Europe in the fifth millennium B.C. Caesar fought the barbarian Gauls (also called Indo-Europeans) just before the birth of Jesus.

Four thousand years is a very long period of time for an invasion to occur. This is a very interesting concept for me. The implication to historians is that it wasn't people invading so much as it was ideas. The term 'Indo-Europeans' does not, and cannot, represent a specific group of people of one genetic and cultural stock. Instead it represents an idea, whose name is patriarchy. Patriarchy didn't happen all over the world at once. It had a long interface with what came before.

So, in some ways, we are back to that 'short and brutish life' of Gordon Child, as the new historians' view of prehistoric life in that time before the written word. But something happened on this Earth—in that time shortly before the written word—that changed everything. It was called agriculture.

Koster

Koster is an archaeological site in Western Illinois dug under the direction of Stuart Struever of Northwestern University. He began this dig in 1969 as a single one-metre-square test pit and it has ended up as one of the most important archaeological sites in North America. Struever found artifactual evidence from as early as 8000 BC up to 1600 AD. While the Koster site is in the United States, lower levels speak clearly of that time when humans were still hunter-gatherers. From their point of view, the introduction of agriculture—which can be seen in the higher layers in the dig—wasn't a great success. The earlier hunter-gatherers lived longer, healthier lives in their non-defended communities. Of most interest, they spent fewer hours a day collecting their hugely diversified sources of food from Nature than their progeny, the early agriculturalists, who had to spend untold hours tilling the fields, sowing the seed, and weeding. As a result, hunter gatherers had more leisure time. Agriculture meant more work.

Perhaps it is the time of the interface between the hunter-gatherers and the farmers that we are really talking about.

Goddess and the New Historians

Goddess suffers under these new archaeologists. Actually, the old giants like Glyn Daniel and Gordon Child had little difficulty with the concept of a Goddess/high priestess, and her son, lover, consort. The

Matriarchal concept first came into academic consciousness in the nineteenth century with the works of Johann Bachofen (*Das Mutterrecht* in 1861), and Lewis Henry Morgan, an American anthropologist in his *American Society* in 1877. Morgan based his research on the American Indian. In the Iroquois Confederation, for example, women are held in high esteem. They choose the chiefs and decide if their people are to go to war. In European mythology, many of the oldest tales speak of matrifocal kinds of governance. Bachofen wrote of Menelaus becoming King of Sparta by marrying Helen (indicating that the line of succession to the throne came through women), but look what happened to Helen when she ran away with Paris.

But what about the over-abundance of female figurines at Marija Gimbutas' digs? First, a question of interpretation. How do you decide which figurines are male, and which are female? Some are obvious. Ones with testicles and penis are male, and pregnant ones, and ones with breasts are female. That's clear, but how do you decide the gender of figurines that don't have either phalluses or obvious breasts? Is a triangle in the groin area a pubic patch or a loin cloth? Also, Gimbutas mentions the fact that at many of the sites where she found these figurines, there were also, in roughly similar numbers, phallic shaped stones—but she doesn't talk much about them.

I think Ronald Hutton's most telling observation about these figurines has to do with their purported use. Who says that just because you find a female figurine of 6000 BC, that it is a representation of Goddess? If three thousand years from today, they dug into the American culture, they might claim that we were a Goddess centered culture as well because the vast majority of figurines from the Twentieth Century, like those of Old Europe, would be female.

And the Goddess' name was Barbie—with her lover, consort, son Ken.

As I listen to Ronald Hutton and other new archaeologists and historians, it is clear that they feel there really is no solid evidence to suggest there ever was a time when Goddess held sway. It almost feels like some of these new archaeologists take delight in "proving" that men always held the upper hand.

The Goddess on Crete

Margaret Ehrenberg is an academic archaeologist and anthropologist who has taught at colleges and universities on both sides of the Atlantic and has written a book, *Women In Prehistory*. She posits that one way of developing ideas about how our hunter-gatherer foremothers and fathers interrelated is to look at those cultures today that still gain their sustenance that way. Ehrenberg reveals her bias when she says of them, "Most *serious* scholars have seen that there are no societies today where women are regularly in the prime positions of leadership, and consequently question whether matriarchy could ever have existed." (Ehrenberg. 1989. p.63—my italics.) My concern is with her use of the word 'serious'. What is she trying to say here? 'Serious' equals academically acceptable? Feminist herstorians are not "serious"? Somehow, the use of this word denigrates the work of so many of the new thinkers in the field of prehistory.

On top of that, these 'serious scholars' have unfortunately missed the point. Most recent serious feminist herstorians today do not claim that there ever was a time of matriarchy—a time when women had control, dominance, and power over men. Many feminist writers like Riane Eisler and Marija Gimbutas feel that women just do not and did not work that way, so the word they use is 'matrifocal' or 'gylany'. These concepts are quite different from the word 'matriarchal'.

In the early chapters, Ehrenberg herself (unlike her more 'serious' colleagues) does support the notion of gylany, but she puts the appearance of what she calls 'androcentricity' in the mid-Neolithic—much earlier than the last vestiges of Goddess herstorians find at Knossos and Troy. In a way, both these times—from the mid-Neolithic to Knossos and Troy—mark the beginning and end of the transition from gylany to patriarchy. It's the cusp. While Ehrenberg covers the entire spectrum of prehistory, I would like to focus on her thoughts about Minoan Crete, as that civilization is said by herstorians to have been one of the last vestiges of open Goddess worship in the Eastern Mediterranean.

As far as a Goddess-centered culture on the island of Crete is concerned, in terms of the many frescoes of the Minoan Civilization at Knossos, Ehrenberg argues, "...although it may be possible to gain some insight into women's roles from the activities in which they are portrayed, the mere fact of pictures of women certainly can not be used as evidence of high status. In our own society, for instance, pictures of women—even naked large-breasted women, for which we find parallels in Minoan art—predominate in certain magazines and newspapers, in advertising and the like. But these images are created entirely for the pleasure of men, and far from reflecting female dominance, they are actually symptomatic of the low status of women in our society." (Ehrenberg. 1989. p.111)

Aside from the fact that these thoughts are blatantly ethnocentric, Ehrenberg's analogy doesn't follow. She's talking about *Playboy* magazine or Page Three of *The Sun*—both of which are usually read in the privacy of one's bedroom. These Minoan frescoes are found on the walls of the palace/temple of the ruler of one of the major civilizations of the Bronze Age in the Mediterranean. To make Ehrenberg's analogy work, we must look at the walls of the White House, Buckingham Palace or the Vatican where the only "naked large-breasted women" might be found in a Renaissance painting or perhaps on a statue of Britain's warrior Queen Boadicea. These certainly don't denigrate women. Ehrenberg's analogy just doesn't work.

Ehrenberg ends up saying of the women of Crete, "Even if we may hypothesize that women, or at least women of higher status, may have had a better deal in Minoan Crete than in many other later societies, it is impossible to argue that they actually held power." (Ehrenberg, 1989. p.118) Remember that power actually isn't the issue here: it is Goddess worship versus the patriarchy.

Ehrenberg seems to be taking the approach throughout her discussion of Crete that because she can't find archaeological evidence that proves conclusively that women did have power (and I'm not exactly sure what that evidence would be), it proves that they probably didn't have it. The fact that there were many frescoes of women at Knossos doesn't necessarily lead one to the assumption that women were of low status either.

Continuing with the denigration of Goddess by present day historians, they also tell us that references to a mother Goddess appear only in rather late texts in Sumeria and Anatolia. In Egypt, the Earth was masculine. In Malta, new archaeologist David Trump has shown that while some of the figurines were clearly female, the large cult statues with kilts actually had no breasts, and appeared to be androgenous. The long-standing thought that the underground temples were in the shape of the Goddess was shown not to be the case. Apparently the evidence now shows that the prehistoric citizens of Malta had actually experimented over the years with building circular forms, and had settled on the 'hourglass' as one of the best. It had nothing to do with Goddess. It goes on and on like this. In many cases historians take the same evidence that herstorians use to prove that their view is correct! There are several examples in this paragraph alone! Looking at these kilted androgenous figures, herstorians would see evidence of gylany. The hourglass is our old friend the labrys. To paraphrase American author Lew Wallace, reality (as well as beauty) seems to be in the eye of the beholder.

The Eye Of the Beholder

In the discussion of whose vision of the past is correct, let's not miss the forest for the trees. Today, many people including myself are feeling the total over-dominance of a certain form of consciousness on the Earth—one that is based on power-over, competition, and the survival of the fittest militarily, athletically and economically, in all fields. There is now a call for another way. The academically-acceptable Goddess stories of our youth struck a concordant note. Why haven't we heard more about Her? Regardless of what went on in prehistory—in *history*—there has been a constant suppression of the feminine. From the Patriarchs of Israel and the misogynist Saul/Paul of the New Testament, through the witch persecutions and the Industrial Revolution, Western societies have found ways of devaluing the female (in all of us). Through the last two millennia, the Christian Church, and most of the other world religions for that matter, have been stalwart ongoing supporters of this patriarchal outlook.

How About Balance?

Now there is a calling for something new. But what is it? Goddess needs to be there in balance with God. Ultimately, it doesn't really matter whose view of prehistory is correct. The point is that we need to find ways of allowing more female, receptive, birth-giving, intuitive energy into our lives today without, at the same time, throwing out all the benefits that the rational scientific mind has brought us. It's not an either/or model. It's both the intuitive and the rational. Both Goddess and God.

This is one of the concerns I have about Riane Eisler's vision of the future as gylany. There is another word that has been around for quite some time that means, supposedly, exactly the same thing. It's *androgyny*. The *an* of gylany is the *andro* of *androgyny*. *Andro* = man. The *gy* of androgyny is the *gy* of gylany—both come from the same root: Gaia, the primal Greek Goddess. Both words mean the same thing, a mixture of male and female, but when historians use the word androgyny—the man comes first. Herstorians use gylany—the woman comes first. I want a tie. I seek a place where the rational and the intuitive work together—as equals. We need a word that doesn't put *matri-* or *patri-* first. How about *panarchy*? Or *gnowing*?

Chicken or Egg?

In different areas of the Earth Mysteries, the question of which came first comes up. Were women and

Goddess here before our present male patriarchy? Does the building of a sacred site draw the Earth Energies, or are the energies there first? (I go with the latter.) But then there is the question of the maze and the labyrinth? Which came first?

For me, the resolution to this question is now clear. The labyrinth came first. Its roots go way back into mesolithic times. The Greeks used the word 'labyrinth' in their Theseus myth because that was the word they heard the Minoans use in their earlier myth. Of course in the earlier Minoan myth, it really was a labyrinth—a way to get to Goddess. The Greeks described a maze, but incorrectly called it a labyrinth because they had not yet made a distinction between the two.

There is a circular Classical Seven Circuit Labyrinth made of stones on St. Agnes, one of the Scilly Isles West of Cornwall in South-Western England. While its original builder is debatable, by the mid 1980's it had fallen into disrepair. Stones had been kicked about and were not put back because people had forgotten what the original labyrinth had looked like. At the entrance there were three choices, not the single path. The center had turned into spiral. The labyrinth had degenerated into a maze. I think this is how it happened all along the line. Even though Pharaoh Amenemhatan's Egyptian maze goes back to c.1795 BC (I suspect that it was an early intentional maze), I believe that labyrinths, by perhaps tens of thousands of years, came first, and mazes—degenerate forms to amuse and confuse—came later.

Lessons in Gnowing

There have not been any Lessons in Gnowing for the last several chapters because the final chapter, *Modern Uses*, is an ongoing lesson in gnowing. As you read the final chapter, I urge you to try to pick one of the examples to really work on (at least at first). You probably won't use all of the suggestions, but look for the one that appeals to you the most, and give it a solid try.

CHAPTER TEN

MODERN USES

"Labyrinths draw you in when you study them."—John Michell

OVER THE YEARS, I'VE FOUND, or developed, quite a few uses for labyrinths, these magical unicursal mazes. They can aid in meditation, be used as a tool to make vows with, or to begin and end ceremonies. Often my feet have been called to run them. (When running—especially good on turf mazes as they offer banked tracks—try throwing your arms in the air and closing your eyes when you reach the center/goal.) Labyrinths can enhance any solitary moving meditation. Just walking the circular paths with the mind in neutral is a meaningful activity. People meditate for all kinds of different reasons: from stress reduction and self-awareness, to seeking Cosmic consciousness. It is the function of sacred space to enhance any spiritual activity. Walking meditatively in a space like a labyrinth enhances the possibility of your achieving whatever it is that you are meditating for.

It is interesting how easily one can become lost in a labyrinth when it is being used as a tool for meditation. It's a strange feeling. As you become lost in thought, it's also possible to become lost in the labyrinth, "Where am I?" By definition, that's not supposed to happen in a labyrinth, and yet it's happened to me quite often. One finds oneself by losing oneself. While meditation in a labyrinth is a valid use, for me their power lies in their ability to be very powerful problem solving devices and tools of spiritual growth.

Problem Solving

I have found that the paths of the Classical Seven Circuit Labyrinth can be very useful in working with all kinds of difficulties in my life. In Chapter Eight, *Mirrors*, I introduced the chakras and their relationship to these seven paths. I used key words for each path: Root—Physical, Sacral—Emotional, Solar—Mental, Heart—Personal Spiritual, Throat—Manifestation, Brow—Vision, Crown—God/dess. Let's take a closer look at these in the order that you will encounter them in the labyrinth (3-2-1-4 / 7-6-5-8) in terms of their ability to aid the seeker in solving problems.

Stand at the mouth of the labyrinth. Think of a problem.

66. Labyrinth with the paths numbered

JEFF SAWARD/CAERDROIA

The first path is:

3. Mental—"I think…". As you walk this path, the issue is what do you think about the problem? What does your left brain have to say about this concern? There is a tendency among some to never use the word "problem", but instead use "opportunity". The labyrinth works just as well for an opportunity as it does for a problem. The task on this first path is to think about it.

2. Emotional—"I feel…". As you turn the corner from path three to two, your focus switches from: what do you think about the problem/opportunity to, how do you feel about it? What kinds of emotions are brought up when you contemplate this issue? Does it make you sad? Happy? Fearful? Is there a pit in your stomach? How do you feel about it? If nothing comes up, use "I feel" as a mantra. As you walk path two, with each step, over and over again say, "I feel, I feel…" The emotions are there. They will come when called forth.

1. Physical—"How will this problem/opportunity effect me on the physical level?" Will I have enough money? What will happen to the things that I own? How will it affect my body? You've already dealt with what you think about it, and how you feel. This is the path where you look at the physical world. It is the longest path. We spend most of our energy dealing with this "reality". It extends from one unfortunate extreme of, "Will my children have enough to eat today?" to an absurd other of, "Will I be able to afford a new mink coat this year?". Both are physical level issues.

4. Personal Spiritual—"How will this problem/ opportunity affect *my* spiritual life?" This is not asking you to look at the present spiritual state of the Christian Church, or of the people in your community. It looks at your own personal relationship with the Great Mystery. "Will I grow closer to the One if I do this? Or, is what I'm doing actually impeding my spiritual growth?" This level may not be very relevant to some, but it is quite necessary for others. It gives you the chance to explore how this quandary is affecting your personal spiritual growth.

7. God/dess—"Oh, Great Spirit/God/Allah/Goddess/Cerridwen/ St. Michael (*i.e.* your deity of choice) be with me." This is the path of invocation to that deity towards which you personally aspire. It's the shortest path. As we spend most of our time dealing with issues in the physical world, we (most of us anyway) spend the least amount of our time on this seventh path, in conscious communication and awareness of our Maker. This is the path to call for Her/His help.

The Critical Turn:

6. Vision—There's not really a question for the next two paths (six and five), it is more an attitude of openness. Up until now, on each path, it was some aspect of your consciousness that instigated the response to the various questions. At this corner, at the beginning of path number six, you have to let go and let God/dess. The answers on the next two paths come from your intuition rather than from your analytical mind. They come from the Deity that you invoked. And the most important thing to gnow is that

answers *do* come. It can be a picture of the solution in your mind's eye. A flash. A few words.

While I have called this point "Vision", it doesn't necessarily mean that you will *see* an answer to your problem. You may hear it. You may feel it. You may just sense it, but in one way or another, you will gnow an answer.

Go with the first answer. Don't say to yourself, "Oh no, I don't like that one, give me something else." You will get something else—but it won't be as useful. When working with the intuition, learn to trust that first hit. The more you do, the more accurate you'll get.

5. Manifestation—"What is the first step?" OK, you received a possible solution. What is the first thing that you have to do to bring that particular solution to fruition or manifestation? What is the first thing you need to do to make it happen? Again, an answer will come to you. Listen with your inner ear. Trust the process, and open to your intuition.

This "first step" is the critical point in working magic. What is that very first physical thing that will show me that my idea is real? This shows that spirit has descended into matter. Manifestation.

8. Goal—This is basically an intermediate rest stop in this process. It also marks the switch from taking in information to evaluating it. Take some time here to relax, take a few deep breaths, and turn around and walk the process backwards. This last half is the evaluative part of the process, and just as important as the first half.

Going Out:

5. Manifestation—Look at the specific first step that your intuition gave you on the way in. Don't judge it, just look at it.

6. Vision—See the answer to the problem/opportunity your intuition gave you on the way in. Again don't be judgmental, just look at what you have already been shown on this path. 'Re-vision' it.

7. God/dess—Give thanks to your Deity of choice for bringing you this awareness and this possible solution.

Now Get Critical and Judgmental:

4. Personal Spiritual—How will this solution affect your spiritual life? If you do that, will you ultimately grow spiritually? If you implement that first step, and that leads to the vision/solution you had, will it bring you closer to the One?

1. Physical—How will this solution affect you on the physical level? Will you have what you want? Will you have enough? Will your body suffer? If what you envisioned actually transpires, how will it work for you on the physical level? Will it bring you more money? Is that what you really need?

2. Emotional—How do you feel about this solution? Is there a twinge in your stomach? Does it make you feel good? Are you anxious? Looking forward to it? Do you feel it's a good way to resolve the issue?

3. Mental—What do you think about this solution? It is important to remember that no divinatory method is always correct. Sometimes real baloney comes through. You probably have seen the pastel rainbow New Age types with that faraway look on their faces who come up with some *non sequitur* like, " I know I said I'd help at the festival, but Spirit has told me to move to Tasmania. I'm leaving tomorrow. Isn't it wonderful?"

Your left brain, your rational mind is the first and the last to deal with this problem/opportunity. It has to agree as well. If there's been some static on the air waves, and you've received bullshit instead of a real workable resolution, the mental path might well be the path that sees it. It has to work on all the levels/paths. Gnowing works through consensus.

An Example

That's the process of how to use the Classical Seven Circuit Labyrinth as a problem solving device. Let's take a specific issue to see how it works. You can ask any question you want when you pause at the mouth of the labyrinth. It can be very general like, "How am I doing in my life right now?" Or it can be specific like, "My wife and I have not been getting along. She says I don't help enough around the house, and she thinks my interest in things esoteric is a bit crazy, though sometimes she seems interested. I've just received an offer of a job in California that will give me twice the salary, but since my wife has a good

job here, she probably won't come. Should I accept the job?"

Let's work with this specific question. Go to the mouth of the labyrinth and restate the question. "Should I accept the job in California?" Walk into the labyrinth.

3. Mental—"What do I think about moving to California?" Well, I think it's definitely a promotion in my career. I think it's in a part of the country that I have not been to and the change might do me good. I think my wife probably won't come with me. Keep up with the "I thinks" until you reach the turn to path.

2. Emotional—"How do I feel about going to California?" I feel excited about the offer. If my wife doesn't come, I feel I'll miss her. I love her, but we fight so much. I feel…, I feel…, I feel…

1. Physical—"What will it be like for me on the physical level if I move to California?" It's warm and sunny out there. The company has offered me a house. It's not very big, but with my salary, I'll be able to fix it up. I'll have to fix all my meals and keep the place cleaned up. I'm not very good at that.

4. Personal Spiritual—"How will moving to California affect my spiritual life?" I'll be able to really get into some different spiritual practices. I hear that there are all kinds of spiritual groups out there. This could really be an opening for me!

7. God/dess—"Oh Great Mystery be with me."

6. Vision—"What should I do?" *Don't go!* Now this might not be the answer you were expecting, but for this trip through the labyrinth, go with it, do *not* say

something to yourself like "No, I want another answer." Accept and work with the first thing your intuition brings you so it will learn that you strive for the truth the first time every time.

5. Manifestation—"What is the first thing I should do?" *Do more at home!* Again, this may not be exactly what you expected or wanted to hear, but go with it.

8. Goal. Take a few moments to relax. Don't get in to what the last two paths have brought you, just breathe deeply. When you're ready, turn around and walk back to:

5. Manifestation—As you walk this path, just remember "Do more at home." Envision yourself doing that.

6. Vision—Hear that message that came through so loud and clear, "Don't go!" If there's time, hear the message again, "Don't go!"

7. God/dess—"Thank you Lord and Lady, for that revelation."

4. Personal Spiritual—It is at this point that you become judgmental. "What will happen to your spiritual life if you don't go?" Well, I would have to find ways of encouraging my wife to feel more comfortable with my interest in things spiritual. When we do connect on these levels, it's so beautiful.

1. Physical—"How will staying home affect me on the physical level?" The first step was to "Do more at home.". We'll have less money, but perhaps if I can specifically schedule more time working on the house

and helping with the chores, my wife, the woman I really do love, will then have more time, and perhaps feel more inclined to look in to spiritual issues in her own life.

2. Emotional—"How do I feel about the notion of staying here?" I must admit that one reaction is disappointment. However, I've become aware again how much I really do love my wife even though we have been having some trouble recently. I don't feel great about doing more of the household chores, but I also know that deep down I've been feeling guilty for not doing my share of the work.

3. Mental—"And finally, what do I think about the notion of staying here and working it out?" I think I will lose my wife if I go, and I know now that I do not want to lose her. I think if I can really get involved in helping around the house, really cutting down on the time my wife has to spend on household chores, I believe that we will be able to find a way to work this out.

At the mouth of the labyrinth, turn around and face the center, and offer thanks for what has happened. Now, you may not have answered those questions exactly in these ways—everyone is different, but it ought to give you a good idea how the process feels.

Nothing says that you must always follow your intuition. But the labyrinth is a tool that can help you look at issues in your life from many points of view. It's holistic—a way of gnowing.

While the above exercise works best—especially for beginners—if you have a labyrinth big enough to physically walk through, and best of all, if it is also on an Earth energy power center, this isn't absolutely necessary. You can also draw one, and very slowly follow the path with your finger.

Now You Try It

Why don't you try this right now? Using the labyrinth on this page, think of an issue that you're working with presently in your life. Now, you need to form a question. Take your time in forming it. Think your way through the problem/opportunity, and the right question will be there. Be precise. When you're ready, put your finger at the mouth of the drawing, and ask the question. Follow the paths, and see what happens. You might be surprised at the specificity and by the quality of the answers. It might be helpful if you make and use a crib sheet for the first five or ten times you use the Classical Seven Circuit Labyrinth for problem/opportunity solving. It looks something like this (Fig. 67).

Take some time now to think of an important issue in your life. What's your biggest hassle?... What came to your mind when you read that last sentence? Work with that one. Using the above crib sheet, slowly "walk" the labyrinth with your finger. Please try this now...

It is confusing to use this process at first. The crib sheet really helps beginners, but you will find that after the first six or seven uses, you won't need it any more.

JEFF SAWARD/CAERDROIA

State the Question

In	Out
3. I think…	**5.** Envision the first step
2. I feel…	**6.** See the Vision
1. The physical	**7.** Thank you God/dess
4. Personal spiritual	**4.** Personal spiritual
7. God/dess	**1.** The physical
6. The Vision	**2.** I feel…
5. The first step	**3.** I think…
8. Breathe	

67. *Problem/opportunity solving with the Classical Seven Circuit Labyrinth*

Deviceless

When you have walked the labyrinth in a conscious manner frequently enough so that you no longer have to check the crib sheet to determine which path you're on—when you *gnow* this process—you're ready to get rid of the tool. Dowsers call this "going deviceless", and it is the goal of the spiritual dowser. What good are physical tools on the other side anyway?

I first met the deviceless labyrinth one day when I was driving my car on an Interstate Highway and found myself working on a problem. As I had been using the turf labyrinth in my front yard just that morning, I thought, wasn't it too bad that I couldn't be there to use the labyrinth now? I could "see" it in my mind. I knew the order of the paths, but how would I know when to turn? The answer was quite simple—I turn to the next path when I find that my mind has wandered from the specific question of that path. When I find myself thinking of something else, I turn on to the next path. I've used this deviceless system with great success. It's just a good way to deal with problems that makes sure that I've looked at the issue from many different points of view. It's a powerful tool.

The Labyrinth in Ceremony: Handfasting

My partner, Linda Cameron, and I are not married. When we decided to live together, we wanted to have some sort of ceremony to mark our coming together, but neither of us wanted to get married. We didn't want to have children (I have two already, and as a teacher/principal Linda spends lots of time with children,

and just doesn't want any of her own). Also, according to some statistics I'd seen, over fifty percent of all marriages end in divorce. I didn't like the odds with marriage. Neither did Linda. We also didn't see any reason why the Church or the State had to have any part in our private agreement. Freddy and Anji, some mutual friends in England, put it all together for us when they asked us, "So when are you two going to be handfasted?"

Handfasting is an ancient Celtic and Gipsy custom where a couple cut their wrists, bind them together, and pledge to walk the same path together for a year and a day. At that time you seriously renegotiate. Either party has the right to drop out of the agreement at that anniversary. It keeps you on your toes.

Handfasting felt right for us. While we didn't slash our wrists and have our blood mingle, we used a ribbon that all of our guests had signed, as witnesses, to tie our wrists together. And we used the labyrinth/turf maze on our front lawn to verbalize out-loud to each other and to our friends where we stood as far as this handfasting was concerned.

"What do we think about this handfasting?"

"How do we feel about it?"

"How will it affect us on the physical level?"

"How will this handfasting affect our spiritual lives?"

"Oh, Great Mystery, God and Goddess be with us."

We then shared our vision for this union, and the first step to manifest that vision. (For me it was based on being truthful.)

On the way out, we spoke about how we felt

68. Sig and Linda's handfasting using a labyrinth

about our visions *vis à vis* each other. The labyrinth was a wonderful way for us to make our feelings and our vows to each other known also to our friends who witnessed it.

After a year and a day (thirteen cycles of the Moon plus one day equals 365 days), we spent the day renegotiating. We went out into the woods and built an altar, and then spent an hour alone writing notes and concerns. Then we came together and shared our thoughts with each other. At the end of the day we again walked our turf labyrinth on our front lawn and made our new vows to each other. Try it. You'll like it.

The Medicine Wheel

I've spoken earlier of Twylah Nitsch, my Seneca Indian Grandmother (a term of respect) and Wolf Clan Mother. Twylah's Grandfather, Moses Shongo, taught her the Seneca traditions when she was a child, before she was taken off the reservation at the age of

six or seven to live in ultimately many different white homes to be Christianized. She was baptized many times because each Christian family she lived with wanted to feel that they had set a heathen soul on the True Path. But Twylah never lost her Grandfather's teachings, and today she shares them with many. Grandmother Twylah (her name is Yehwehnode in Seneca) doesn't care what color your skin is, she cares what color your heart is. My children, Lucas and Jordan, and I are honored to be members of the Wolf Clan and the Seneca Historical Society.

I had been working on the labyrinth for several years when Grandma Twy invited me to go out there and give a workshop on the labyrinth and to make one in her back yard. We decided to make this one rectangular like the Hopi ones.

On the other hand, most of what Twylah teaches has to do with the circle. This circle is the Medicine Wheel. Each Native American Tribe or Nation uses different animals to represent different clans within the wheel. Twylah divides the circumference of the wheel up into twelve sections. Each of the sections, or points on the Medicine Wheel, speak of a very specific way of relating to the truth. She calls the whole process the 'cycles of truth.' Here are the various steps one takes on the cycle of truth:

The Cycles Of Truth

1. **Learn** the truth of what has happened.

2. **Honor** the lessons/knowledge of the experience. (Acknowledge what we experience.)

3. **Accept** the lesson. This is not always the easiest thing to do. **Accept** the responsibility for having made this choice. **Accept** the changes coming with that choice.

4. **See**/perceive the inner potential for the posi-

tive/good that may come from the experience.

5. **Hear**/harmony. We are always exactly where we are supposed to be.

6. Trust our **faith**. Know that we will grow.

7. **Love** unconditionally. **Love** ourselves unconditionally.

8. Intuition **serves** to help us find within what we need to find right now.

9. **Will** to live. Live **will** through truth.

10. **Work** creatively. It's the best way to be productive, to provide for personal needs, and to take our minds off things. A redefinition of "**work**" may be necessary.

11. **Walk** in truth. **Walk** tall. Use magnetism to attract positive energy and to release what isn't needed.

12. Give **thanks** for healing and becoming whole. Unite (our gifts) with those who love us.

We thank our teachers and our guides.

(*Clan Destiny*, Summer 1988, p. 14. © Twylah Nitsch)

69. The Seneca Wolf Clan Medicine Wheel —The Cycles of Truth

One of the ways the Medicine Wheel is used is with overlays. These show the seeker different ways of relating to the wheel. Twylah overlays the Cycles of Truth on top of her rectangular labyrinth. As she enters all medicine wheels from the East, and the mouth of her labyrinth faces that direction, it is relatively easy to line up:

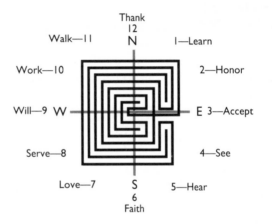

70. Twylah's Labyrinth and the Cycles Of Truth

As you walk the paths, the cross and the 90° turns let you know exactly where you are on the Cycles of Truth Medicine Wheel. Instead of working it by which path you are on, you work it by where you are on each path. The square shape of this labyrinth aids in this. Again, you can work with a specific problem, or you can do a general reading like, "How am I doing now in my life?"

Planetary Questions

One of the subjects that I have been interested in over the last three or four years is archaeoastrology—how did the ancients in their stone rings or Medicine Wheels work with the planets that they saw in the heavens? As we have seen, the labyrinth represents the planet Mercury quite well. It also dances quite well with all the visible planets. Kelley Hunter, an astrologer friend of mine, pointed out to me that just as there are seven paths, there are seven visible planets in our Solar system. Normally, the Earth isn't included, but when it is, this allows the Sun to be at the goal, and Saturn, the outermost visible planet, to be on path one. If the planets are then listed in order of how close they come to the Sun, (the Moon gets closer to the Sun than the Earth ever does), it looks like this:

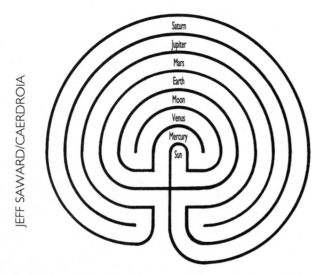

JEFF SAWARD/CAERDROIA

71. The planetary paths

On several occasions, when groups I have been working with come together for a week or more, we have worked together towards a chance for all participants to meet themselves and the planets.

Planet Masks

The Oak Dragon Project runs nine-day camps out in farmers' fields near sacred sites in Britain. At one of our camps that was based on the theme of Spiritual Traditions, we organized a planetary labyrinth that was a rite of passage. At the beginning of our time together, we asked who might be interested in being one of the planets at a ceremony at the end of the week. We chose the specific people by lots. This group got together throughout the week to make their specific planet masks and to get other parts of their costumes together. We also spent a great deal of time initially talking about the astrological aspects of each planet.

For example, Mars is red and represents activity, assertiveness, making things work out, etc. That person spent time getting in to that energy. It helped each planet have a better idea about what their mask would look like, what color they wanted to paint it, and what costume they would need. When each person had a good idea of what their specific planet was about, they made their mask.

One way to make masks is out of gauze cloth impregnated with the kind of plaster used to make casts for broken legs. It is available at most pharmacies or chemists. Put a little Vaseline on the person's face first. Then wet the plaster strips and put them on the face making sure to leave a hole at the nostrils for breathing. Three or four layers will make it strong enough. When it's dried just a little bit, slowly peel the mask off (it's a very weird feeling), and add any plaster or other features that will enhance the meaning of that planet. Allow them to dry—hair dryers speed this process up, the Sun works well too. Then paint the masks to match the character of the planet you are trying to represent. All this requires that some of the people making the masks know something about astrology. This will usually not be a problem because astrologers will be attracted to making planetary masks in the first place.

Death in the Afternoon

Two days before the planetary walk, we had a camp-wide gathering called "Death in the Afternoon". In a guided visualization, we all reviewed our lives—much like one hears of someone doing in the time between jumping off a cliff and hitting the ground. What have you done well? Of whom would you ask forgiveness? Who would you forgive? What would you have done differently? What will you be remembered for? Other questions of this nature were explored by all of the participants.

Suddenly, there was a high shrill scream. We were "dead". We then walked slowly down to a near-by stream where we were individually blindfolded, spun around several times to make us dizzy, and taken to Annwn, the Celtic underworld, symbolized by a small shrine by the stream.

That evening, as we were dead, we went to visit our ancestors at Wayland's Smithy, a neolithic long barrow several miles from our camp. It was cool and clear. The stars were out in great profusion. Someone had placed a candle at the back of the chamber that went in to the Eastern end of the long barrow. We didn't talk, and each of us spent time thinking about our ancestors. Then each went in, one at a time and—in different ways—communed with them. As we were leaving, the Moon favored us by rising and aligning directly down the chamber of the barrow. It was a magnificent sight.

The next morning we had a "How are you doing?" session. It was amazing how many participants enjoyed being "dead". This was a time when each of us could leave all of life's baggage behind, when we could look at our lives so far, and with the perspective of being "dead" could contemplate changes we might want to make.

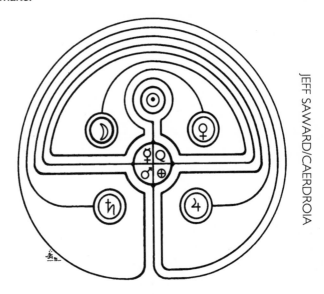

72. The planetary labyrinth: the path and the planetary positions at the turns

That evening, as the mist rose in our field, we were led from the shrine of Annwn (pronounced "ah-noon") to the gates of the planetary labyrinth. There we saw all the planets standing in a row, as in Figure 71, so we could see the order in which they went out from the Sun. At the command of "Planets, go to your stations," they walked to the beginning of their paths.

One at a time, the participants were sent down the winding path to the vesica-shaped boat of Charon the boatman, who for a penny, took dead souls over the river Styx. At the mouth of the labyrinth, Charon asked each soul, "What do you want from your life?"

At each turn in the labyrinth, the appropriate planet was standing there to ask the participant a question which that planet (from an astrological perspective) might ask. The planets were acting as channels for their particular energy. Each participant could theoretically be asked a different question. As they walked each path, the participants contemplated the specific question they had been asked at the beginning of that path. Here is a sampling of what the questions might have been:

The first was Mars. "Are you satisfied with how you are using your energies now?"

Jupiter. "In what ways are you expanding your horizons?"

Saturn. "How are you getting along with your father?"

Earth. "As you walk your path, are you grounded?"

Mercury. "Do you think you are doing the best you can?"

Venus. "How is your love life?"

Moon. "Reflect on your feelings. Are you finding joy?"

The Sun was a mirror. Each participant came to the center and found themselves. Also at the center was a message, a key word, that all participants could use as they went back out on path number five. As it relates to the Moon, it was, "Reflect." (What do you think about all this?)

As the participant came to the end of the lunar path, s/he encountered the Moon. The last gift of this lunar character was to give the participant the key word for the next path (Venus), in this case, "Enjoy." (What does your heart tell you about all this?) And so on out of the labyrinth until at the final turn was Mars who, right in character, said something like, "OK, go for it!"

At the mouth, Charon told everyone the exact time, so if they were interested from an astrological point of view, they could cast a chart for their exact moment of re-birth.

We then took a seat somewhere around the outside of the labyrinth, and waited silently for all to finish. After that, we broke into groups of four to discuss our experience. This was a way of allowing space for each participant to process anything that might have come up for them in the labyrinth in a smaller, less threatening environment.

Finally, we gathered together again as a whole group to sing, "Happy Birthday to Us!" We then went to the camp café to share a meal. Sharing food is an excellent way to ground yourself after a ceremony.

The planetary labyrinth is a painless way for non-astrologers to learn some astrology. The important point is that each planetary character needs to become a conduit for that planet's energy, and their questions will vary depending upon what each participant needs to hear.

73. *Staldon Stone Row, near Cornwood, Dartmoor.*

SIMANT BOSTOCK

Stone Rows:
The Straight Labyrinth?

I have seen stone rows in New England, and in different parts of megalithic Europe. I have seen them in Sweden, Scotland, England and France. I followed a single row stretching over several miles on Southern Dartmoor in South-Western England. Staldon Stone Row in South central Dartmoor, has many stones over six feet high. There are pairs of rows as at Merryvale Stone Rows, also on Dartmoor, or multiple rows as at Carnac in Brittany. The individual stones can be very small—almost swallowed up by the turf—or they can be enormous like at Carnac where at times row after row of behemoth megalithic boulders tower above you.

I have walked stone rows for years wondering what they were used for. One time, a group of us decided to run a pair of rows at Merryvale. Several of us noticed that at various points along the rows it felt as if something, or someone, had blown a burst of air right in our faces. I was looking for the sources of those bursts of wind so intently when I ran it, that I almost ran head on in to the blocking stone at the end of the rows! I've had this same experience at Shovel Down, another series of stone rows on North-Eastern Dartmoor.

You can experience this without running by using your L-rods. Should you find yourself at the end of a stone row, pull out your rods and ask to be shown the row's chakras or nodes. As you walk the row, your rods will stay in the search position, except when you reach a chakra—called a node point—where they will cross. Keep track of the number of points. You will find that there are seven. Stone rows seem to be like straight labyrinths. While I have not used them for problem solving, I suspect that they would work quite well. They're great to use for walking meditations.

Making Temporary Big Labyrinths

The best material to make an outdoor temporary labyrinth with is tennis or football lime. It is sometimes called Guide Lime. A fifty-pound bag costs less than $5.00 (£3.00). Mix it half-and-half with water and apply it on the grass with a dustpan brush. Remember these lines are temporary: they will be gone by the third rain. Be sure not to confuse Guide Lime either with regular garden lime (it disappears into the grass, and doesn't leave a white line), or with slaked lime (the kind of lime used in making cement—it will burn your skin and the grass). You want the stuff they line

tennis courts and football fields with. Indoor labyrinths can be put on carpets with yarn and masking tape. Use your own feet as measures to keep all the paths similar in width. I find two men's feet lengths is about the minimum width if you want people to be able to pass each other.

74. Barbara's Labyrinth

Barbara's Labyrinth and Ceremony

We have already seen the similarity between Barbara's labyrinth and the yearly path of Mercury. This type of labyrinth—where you can come out straight from the middle—has some interesting uses in ceremony. We have used Barbara's labyrinth to begin and end ceremonies. The Tennis court/Guide Lime is good to make it with as you need to walk the line. We walk in the usual way, holding hands in a long chain. Long chains of people in labyrinths are always powerful, and are a simple way to build up the energy. They are even more powerful if you ask everyone to consciously look into the eyes of anyone that they are facing as they go through the paths.

At the beginning, we walk in to the labyrinth—winding ourselves up—and leave from the center to do whatever ceremony we have planned. After the ceremony is over, we again link hands, and go directly to the center of the labyrinth, and walk out—unwinding ourselves after the ceremony is over. Barbara's Labyrinth provides a way to wind up for ceremony and to unwind afterwards.

Chartres

There was a reflowering of labyrinths in the Medieval period. Victorian drawings show monks of the Middle Ages crawling the path of the labyrinth on their knees. This was apparently done as an act of purification and atonement for one's sins, a preparation for later religious ceremonies.

Full-sized, very complex labyrinths from that time can be found, among other places, in Gothic Cathedrals. While labyrinths are not found in all of them, we know that some cathedrals have taken them up or covered them over for various reasons during their history. One was ordered to be destroyed by the cathedral priesthood because children were running it during the service and distracting from what was going on up at the high altar. The labyrinths that remain in Gothic Cathedrals are of greater complexity than the Classical Seven Circuit Labyrinths. However, they also have their patterns that can be used in ways similar to the older Classical Seven Circuit Labyrinths.

Europe in the Middle Ages was very involved in the various crusades to Jerusalem. Many who went saw it as a spiritual journey; they went to free the Holy Land from the pagan infidels. Obviously, everyone couldn't go, but the need for pilgrimage has always been strong in Europe. Chaucer's *Canterbury Tales* (originally published in 1402-1404) tell of various people's need to go on that journey. The Pilgrimage tradition is an old one. Usually, a pilgrimage is a quest. Like the knights of that period questing for the Holy Grail, many common folk went on journeys to visit especially holy sites like Canterbury and Glastonbury in Britain, just as today, many devout Moslems visit Mecca in Saudi Arabia. By going on these pilgrimages, the seeker hoped to grow closer to God. Often, the journey was more meaningful than actually achieving the goal. The same is true with the labyrinth.

But not everyone could leave their homes for such long periods of time. The labyrinths—in French cathedrals at Sens, Poitiers, Bayeux, Amiens and Rheims, and in Italian ones at Lucca, and in San Maria-di-Trastavera in Rome—were used by some as mini-pilgrimages. Some labyrinths are called "Jerusalem". They do take a long time to traverse—especially on the knees. Their complexity made them a far longer pilgrimage than the relatively short jaunt of the Classical Seven Circuit Labyrinth.

Undoubtedly, the most famous of these complex

75. *Sacred Geometry at Chartres*

medieval labyrinths is found on the floor of the nave of Chartres Cathedral, a little west of Paris in France. One could write a book in itself about this one labyrinth, its layout, how it works, and how it fits in to the rest of the cathedral. It is a truly marvellous construction which is today usually densely covered with chairs (too many children having fun during boring services?).

Sacred Geometry—Four, Seven and Twelve

Let's start with some simple work with a straight edge and a compass—the tools of the sacred geometer. Draw a diagonal line anywhere through the Chartres labyrinth except horizontally or vertically (line AF).

With your compass, measure the diagonal of the goal (BD). Pivot your compass at D, and swing it out towards F. It will meet at E, right on a wall. Count the paths from D to E, and from E to F. There are seven paths and walls in DE, and four in EF. Seven and four will prove to be important numbers in this labyrinth at

76. *Classical Seven Circuit Labyrinth*

JEFF SAWARD/CAERDROIA

Chartres. I am aware that there are all kinds of other things that can be found through the use of sacred geometry. The main purpose here is to look into possible uses.

So let's get back to the labyrinth itself. The first thing you will notice is that it divides itself neatly into four quarters. There's the four. Walk the labyrinth with your finger.

With the Chartres labyrinth, you enter into the lower left hand quarter first, and you reach the goal from the lower right-hand quarter, after working your way through the labyrinth in a clockwise direction (from six o'clock all the way around to six o'clock).

The Four

Four had great significance to the medieval mind. Of course, there were the four gospel writers—Luke, John, Mark and Matthew. Often, these four were depicted symbolically—St Luke as a bull, John as an eagle, Mark as a lion, and Matthew as a young man. These animals and the young man are also the symbols of the four fixed signs in the zodiac—Luke/bull/Taurus/Earth, John/eagle/the evolved scorpion of Scorpio/Water, Mark/lion/Leo/Fire, and Matthew/the young water carrier/Aquarius/Air.

According to René Querido, author of *The Golden Age of Chartres: The Teachings of a Mystery School and the Eternal Feminine*, these were the four stages of the Mass: Evangelium—the awakening, Offertory—sacrifice, Consecration—transubstantiation, and Communion—the culmination.

These four quarters can mean any group of four that you might know. The four elements can work well. Since we are at Chartres, let's use the four parts of the Mass, and assign them from the first part, "Awakening", in the first quarter that you enter (the lower left-hand one), "Sacrifice" goes in the upper left hand quarter, "Transubstantiation" in the upper right one, to the last quarter (the lower right-handed one) where "Culmination" will be found.

The first quarter looks at the problem/opportunity from the point of view of, "When did I first become aware of this issue?"

The second quarter looks at the problem from the point of view of, "What will I have to give up to resolve this issue?"

The third quarter looks for change. As The Christ is held by the Catholic Church at the point of transubstantiation to actually become the bread and wine, to bring about any true change, energies must shift on all levels. The old must die and make room for the new. This is the quarter of true magic that can facilitate real understanding and growth. "What is the Vision?"

The fourth quarter looks at the Culmination—"What will it look like if I make these changes as far as this issue is concerned?"

The Seven

Count the number of 180° turns there are in any one quarter. There are seven. The chakras that we have already been working with come to mind. At Chartres, one is also reminded of the Seven Liberal Arts—Grammatica, Dialectica, Rhetorica, Musica, Arithmetica, Geometrica, and Astronomica. The Anthroposophist René Querido suggests that these Seven Liberal Arts formed the basis of study at the

Mystery School at Chartres. Perhaps the medieval users of the Chartres labyrinth devised a way to contemplate these areas of study through the seven turns. However, for the purposes of this one example of how this special labyrinth might be used, I will stick with the chakras. They can be used like the planets at the seven turns to announce the key words for the energy of each chakra, seen within the context of the part of the Mass (Evangelium—the awakening, Offertory—sacrifice, Consecration—transubstantiation, and Communion—the culmination) that governs that quarter. The first 180° turn you reach would be personal spiritual on the Awakening level. It would

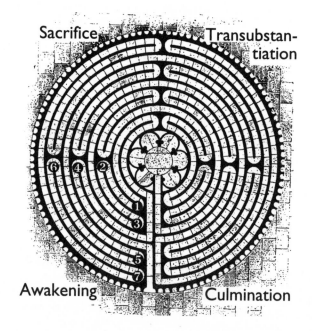

77. The Chartres Labyrinth, the Seven 180° Turns and the Four Parts of the Mass

work that way if you numbered the turns from one to seven starting from the center or from the outermost turn. The question is which way to number them.

Run your finger through the Classical Seven Circuit Labyrinth, and you will notice that you do the outside half of the labyrinth first, and the inside last—just before reaching the goal. On the other hand, with the Chartres Labyrinth, after doing your first 180° turn at Awakening/Personal Spiritual, you basically go inward, and do the inner half of the labyrinth first, and then work your way out to the outer half. It mirrors the Classical Seven Circuit Labyrinth. Therefore, it seems appropriate that the numbering of the 180° turns of the Chartres labyrinth mirror the numbering of the paths of the Classical Seven Circuit Labyrinth.

Let me give you an example here.

On Earth Day, 22 April 1990, I spoke to a group of people at a Timeless Architecture conference in Boston, Massachusetts. After introducing the Classical Seven Circuit Labyrinth, I asked the participants to walk the Chartres labyrinth with this question in mind, "What am I doing to honor the Earth and to help the environment?" The first 180° turn is (A4) Awakening/ Personal/Spiritual. As you walk that path, think about the question, "When did you become aware of the true present state of the Earth on your personal spiritual level? Do you even see it as a spiritual issue at all?"

Then it's on to (S1) Sacrifice on the Physical level. "What do you need to sacrifice on the physical level to bring about the changes necessary to help bring our Earth back into balance?" While there is obviously a very long list of material things that people living in first world countries will have to give up, notice that this path is quite short. Pay attention to the first answers that come to you. They're the ones that are most important for you to sacrifice first.

Which leads you to turn (A1) Awakening to issues of Earth Day. Do you remember when you first became aware of the physical level degradation of our Mother, the Earth?

Then to (A2). "When did you first feel this awareness in your guts?" (For me it happened some years ago when I was driving my car down in New Jersey, just outside of New York City, through what is called "the Jersey flats". It used to be marshland. Now it's one oil refinery or huge holding tank after another, mile after polluted mile. At one point, I drove past one tree, the only one I'd seen for miles. I started to cry. "Hang in there Mother Nature!" I had felt it.)

Then to (A3), "When did you first wake up mentally about the problems our Earth is having?" And on to (S3) and so on...

Walking through the entire Chartres labyrinth will lead you to the final turning point of the heart, *gnowing* what must be done in order to bring about the balance, and then to the goal—Oneness. In terms of Earth Day considerations, this model works very well.

This is a very complicated system. There are various other complicated meditative systems. Most have the same goal—to work your brain so much and so fast that it can't keep up. It goes on overload. It can't handle the complexity, and it just stops functioning. This is just what you've been waiting for—for your mind to shut up. Then the spiritual realizations occur.

This is not to say that your brain will always get overloaded. Sometimes you will get to the goal having looked at an issue from four times seven, or 28 points of view. I would suggest that you walk out of such an exercise with nothing in particular on your mind. Look at the things that come up. Meditate on what has happened to you on the way in.

Lessons in Manifestation:

Making Bigger Labyrinths

The purpose of this book has been to explore ways that the labyrinth can show us more about ourselves and how we are, or are not, functioning in the world. It can help us tune in to our intuition while still retaining the rational analytical skills as well. Not all of the examples are for everyone, but I trust that there was at least one that really resonated with you. Work on that one. Forget the rest (at least for a while).

Also, if my key words for various levels don't work for you, especially if you already have other key concepts that you are using, for God/dess' sake use the ones you already have! There is no "right" way to use these magical tools. The important thing is to continue to use them. If you live in the city, perhaps you could get permission to build a labyrinth in a public park. If not, you can always use a labyrinth drawn on a piece of paper, and walk it with your finger.

In the country, the possibilities of making and using a full-sized labyrinth are greatly enhanced. If you have land in the country, and if you don't stop to think about it, you will immediately *gnow* where to put it.

You can also build temporary labyrinths at fairs and other gatherings. Inside, labyrinths can be made on the floor with yarn and masking tape. They're relatively rugged, and they come up easily.

Outside, I have used both bamboo sticks and yarn as well as tennis court lime. You need about 400 eight-inch bamboo sticks. I get mine in garden stores where longer bamboo sticks are sold to hold up garden plants. Cut them to the proper length. You will also need one or two skeins of yarn. Both for inside and out, I use 'day-glo' colors: they stick out from the background carpet or lawn better than Earth tone yarns. Start with the center of the cross, and make it exactly as you did on paper. The bamboo sticks should be about a foot apart, and the paths should be at least two human foot lengths wide—better three or four.

Be ready to get confused. This seems to be an integral part of the construction of labyrinths. At some point in the construction of most of the many labyrinths I've built, the group, including myself, has become confused. Just keep at it, and you will muddle through perfectly. Confusion seems to be a given factor in their construction.

My personal favorite temporary outdoor labyrinth construction material is tennis court lime as described in "Making Temporary Big Labyrinths" earlier in this chapter. The lime mixes very easily with water, and most labyrinths don't need more than two buckets full (half lime/half water). It is very inexpensive, and washes away after several rainstorms. The best kind of brush to use is a dustpan brush with a long handle. It's easier on your back, and you can see where you are within the labyrinth more easily when standing up. If you make a mistake, wash it away with water and your hand. You may have to touch up this kind of labyrinth after a heavy rainstorm, but it is well worth that small effort. The bamboo sticks do have a nasty habit of hitting ankle bones—especially while running, or in a crowded labyrinthine dance, but for a temporary labyrinth, sometimes they are more acceptable to the landowner as after the event is over, they leave absolutely no trace at all.

Permanent Labyrinths

Permanent labyrinths can be made of many different materials. I'd use tennis court lime to lay it out initially. Stones and small boulders make good walls when they are in plentiful local supply. If possible, they should be the size of a basketball or a bit smaller. I have also seen a cement and tar labyrinth in a school yard in Sweden. They say that the kids run it all the time when they're out in the playground. I set up a labyrinth at a local Waldorf School that used herbs to line the paths.

Any kind of plants in labyrinths require maintenance. The turf maze or lawn labyrinth is a good example of this. My publishers at Gothic Image—Jamie George and Frances Howard-Gordon—helped me several years ago to dig a turf labyrinth in my front lawn. We dug out the path to about six to eight inches down, and the width of our garden shovel, leaving the

The return to the Meander is complete (Sequence drawn by Jeff Saward)

turf to mark the walls. The labyrinth is about 22 feet across, and the paths are surfaced with beach sand. In effect, the runner has a banked track to run on.

The lawn labyrinth is also a piece of Earth art. It's a beautiful sculpture on your lawn. You need to spend an afternoon three times a Summer weeding it. That's a meditation in itself, but it's worth it to have a beautiful problem-solving instrument right on your front lawn!

Labyrinths are really amazing tools. There are so many stories about them and the mythology is rich and deep. They must have been very important to those cultures just before and at the dawn of history. They can be of just as much use to us today in helping us open to our intuition. *Enjoy.*

See the Goddess
Looking to the left,
With Her arms outstretched,
And Her hair swirling 'round Her.

DIANA GRIFFITHS

TIME LINE

BC

c.18,000
-15,000 Meander patterns on Bird Goddesses found in Ukraine

c.15,000 Marks on an Eagle's bone note precisely one full Lunar year

c.5300 Vinca Culture in Old Europe

c.3500 End of Vinca Culture

c.2500 Ionians invade Greece

c.2500 Could be the oldest known Classical Cretan type labyrinth pecked out on a stone slab in Luzzanas, Sardinia (Could also be Iron Age and therefore closer to 500 BC)

c.2000 Minoan Civilization begins in Crete

c.1800
-1300 Val Camonica (Italy) labyrinth and crane dance petroglyphs

c.1795 Pharaoh Amenemhat builds his maze

c.1550 Beginning of Mycenaean/Achaean influence in Crete

c.1500 Thera explodes, the resulting tidal wave weakening the Minoan Civilization

c.1400 Daedalus builds the labyrinth/maze

c.1382 Theseus meets the Minotaur and King Minos

c.1300 Mycenaean/Achaean takeover in Crete complete

c.1270 Greeks go to Troy, ally King Idomeneus of Crete sends 80 ships in support

c.1260 Trojan war (destruction of Troy)

c.1200 Conflagration destroys Knossos

c.1200 Phylos Tablet—rectangular right-hand Classical Cretan Labyrinth (Southern Greece)

c.1100 Dorians invade Greece

c.730 Homer

c.600 Iliad and Odyssey first written down

c.550 Aesop's Fables

500 Dated Cretan coins with the classical Cretan Labyrinth

c.484 Father of History, Herodotus, is born

AD

c.1100 The Zero is introduced as a concept to the West by the Arabs

Middle
Ages The hour of the day becomes important with monks' need to know when to do their various daily services

c.1225 Chartres Cathedral's labyrinth

1655 Oliver Cromwell's horses visit the cathedrals.

c.1830 The minute in timekeeping becomes important with the introduction of railroad schedules.

c.1930 Carl Jung talks about the Shadow.

1970's Feminists begin to talk about revisionist feminist history or 'herstory'.

BIBLIOGRAPHY

Aveni, Anthony F. 1972. 'Astronomical Tables Intended For Use In Astro-Archaeological Studies.' *American Antiquity*, Volume 37, Number 4. The printout itself came from the Department of Physics and Astronomy, Colgate University, Hamilton, New York, USA. Tables for doing ancient astronomy anywhere on the Earth. Some pages have lots of computer glitches.

Bible. The one I used is the Revised Standard Version that first came out in 1952. New York: Thomas Nelson & Sons. Use your favorite version. They all have their particular biases.

Bord, Janet & Colin. 1972. *Mysterious Britain*. London: Garnstone Press. An overview of historic and pre-historic sites that have mysterious stories associated with them. One of the first books that turned me on to the Earth Mysteries.

Bord, Janet. 1976. *Mazes and Labyrinths of the World*. New York: E.P.Dutton & Co. A good overall work. Many excellent photographs. Well researched.

Campbell, Joseph. 1987. *The Masks of God, Vol. I: Primitive Mythology*. New York: Penguin Books. Originally published in 1959.

Champion, Alex. 1990. *Earth Mazes*. 923 Polk Street, Albany, California 94706: Earth Maze Publishing, phone: (415) 527-7990. An American builder of mazes and labyrinths: gives some useful ideas about how they can be used.

Chaucer, Geoffrey. 1986. *Canterbury Tales*. Oxford: Oxford University Press. The ultimate in pilgrimage tales. R-rated.

Cook, Thomas Genn. 1976. *Koster: An Artifactual Analysis Of Two Archaic Phases in Western Illinois*. Evanston, Illinois: Northwestern University Archaeological Program. The transition and comparison between hunter gatherers and farmers.

Dames, Michael. 1976. *The Silbury Treasure*. London: Thames and Hudson. The Goddess at the biggest human- made prehistoric mound in Europe.

Dames, Michael. 1977. *The Avebury Cycle*. London: Thames and Hudson. The Goddess at Avebury. A discussion of Goddess and the various sites in this megalithic complex, and their relevance in the yearly cycle.

Doolittle, Bev. 1989. *Visions: The Art of Bev Doolittle.* Trumbull, Connecticut, USA: The Greenwich Workshop. Faces and figures (simulacra) hidden in paintings.

Downing, Christine. 1988. *The Goddess: Mythological Images of the Feminine.* New York: Crossroads. Good herstory of Ariadne and other maligned Greek Goddesses.

Ehrenberg, Margaret. 1989. *Women in Prehistory.* London: British Museum Publications. A female academic archaeologist and anthropologist's view of the role of women in prehistory.

Eisler, Riane. 1987. *The Chalice and the Blade.* San Francisco: Harper & Row. Revisionist herstory past and future.

Eliot, Alexander (Editor), Joseph Campbell, Mercea Eliade. 1976. *Myths.* New York: McGraw-Hill. Excellent anthology.

Fisher, Adrian, Randoll Coate, and Graham Burgess. 1986. *A Celebration of Mazes.* Saint Albans, Hertfordshire, England: Minotaur Press. A history of mazes including modern variations.

Fisher, Adrian and George Gester. 1990. *The Art of the Maze.* London: Weidenfield and Nicholson. A sumptuously illustrated guide to the mazes and labyrinths of the world.

Gilbert, Harriet. 1987. *A Women's History of Sex.* London: Pandora. A real eye opener.

Gimbutas, Marija. 1982. *The Goddesses and Gods of Old Europe: Myths and Images.* Berkeley, California: University of California Press. 6500—3500 BC evidence of extensive Goddess worship.

Gimbutas, Marija. 1989. *The Language of the Goddess.* New York: Harper & Row. Symbols as language. More evidence of the extent of Goddess worship in prehistory (herstory). Excellent drawings.

Graves, Robert. 1988. *The Greek Myths.* Mount Kisco, New York: Moyer Bell Ltd. Graves has been very influential in reawakening Western Man to Goddess—especially through his powerful book, The White Goddess. The Greek Myths, first published in 1955, is a treasure house of Greek mythology. Well referenced.

Graves, Tom. 1976. *Dowsing—Techniques and Applications.* London: Turnstone Books. (Republished in 1986 as *The Diviner's Handbook* by Thorsons/The Aquarian Press, Northamptonshire, England.) A fine early work of dowsing in sacred space.

Graves, Tom. 1986. *Needles of Stone Revisited.* Glastonbury, England: Gothic Image Publications. A top book on dowsing the Earth energies. A 'must-read'.

Guirand, Felix (Editor). 1959. *Larousse Encyclopedia of Mythology.* New Prometheus Press. One of the standard mythological reference works.

Homer. c.730 BC. *The Odyssey.* New York: P.F.Collier & Son Corporation. Translated by S.H.Butcher and A Lang.

Jaynes, Julian. 1976. *The Origin of Consciousness in the Breakdown of the Bicameral Mind*. Boston: Houghton Mifflin Company. One of the seminal works for me on the intuitive/rational split. Jaynes was fired from Princeton University for writing this book.

Jenkins, Palden. 1987. *Living In Time*. Bath, England: Gateway Books. One of the best books on astrology that I've read. Good both for beginners and those well on the astrological path.

Kraft, John. 1985. *The Goddess In the Labyrinth*. Religionsvetenskaplinga Skrifter Nr 11, Åbo 1985, Åbo Akademi, Sweden. Available from the author at Djäknebergsgatan 3A, 724 021 Västerås, Sweden. Examples of goddesses found in the center of Scandinavian labyrinths with references to many other Indo-European cultures. Can also be ordered from *Caerdroia*, 53 Thundersley Grove, Thundersley, Benfleet, Essex, SS7 3EB, England.

Lonegren, Sig. 1986. *Spiritual Dowsing*. Glastonbury, England: Gothic Image Publications. Dowsing the Earth Energies at sacred spaces, and dowsing and healing.

Lonegren, Sig. 1990. *The Pendulum Kit*. New York: Fireside Books (Simon and Schuster). A good book for beginner dowsers. In part, it combines astrology and dowsing. Comes with pendulum and charts.

Marshack, Alexander. 1972. *The Roots Of Civilization*. New York: McGraw-Hill. The cognitive beginnings of man's first art, symbol, and notation.

Matthews, W.H. 1970. *Mazes and Labyrinths: Their History and Development*. New York: Dover Publications, Inc. (first published in 1922.) Great overall look at the history of mazes/labyrinths. One of the best.

McCrickard, Janet. 1990. *The Eclipse Of the Sun*. Glastonbury, England: Gothic Image Publications. Turns both historians and herstorians on their ears. The earliest myths world-wide speak of the Sun Goddess and the Moon God.

Michell, John. 1975. *The Earth Spirit: Its Ways, Shrines, and Mysteries*. New York: Avon. A delightful view of the Earth mysteries. Good ideas on what these energies might have been used for.

Michell, John. 1979. *Simulacra: Faces and Figures in Nature*. London: Thames and Hudson. Published in the US the same year as: *Natural Likeness, Faces and Figures in Nature*. New York: E.P. Dutton. Natural likenesses at sacred spaces.

Michell, John. 1983. *The New View Over Atlantis*. New York: Harper & Row. First published in a somewhat different version entitled *The View Over Atlantis* in 1969, this is one of the seminal modern books on the subject of the European Earth Mysteries. A must read.

Michelsen, Neil F. (1983). *The American Ephemeris for the 20th Century 1900 to 2000 at Midnight*. P.O. Box 16430, San Diego, California: ACS Publications, Inc. The movements of Mercury—direct and retrograde—came from this book.

Morrison, Tony. 1987. *The Mystery Of the Nasca Lines*. Woodbridge, Suffolk, England: Nonesuch Expeditions Ltd. Good overall book on the figures and the lines. Foreword by Maria Reiche.

Pennick, Nigel. 1986. *Labyrinths: Their Geomancy and Symbolism*. Old England: Runestaff. Labyrinths through history.

Pennick, Nigel. 1990. *Mazes and Labyrinths*. London: Robert Hale. A serious study of the history of mazes primarily in the UK.

Querido, René. 1987. *The Golden Age of Chartres*. Hudson, New York: Anthroposophic Press. In Britain—Edinburgh, Scotland: Floris Books. The teachings of a mystery school and the eternal feminine.

Robinson, James M. (General Editor). 1977. *The Nag Hammadi Library*. San Francisco: Harper & Row. The largest collection of documents of the early Christian heretical sect called the Gnostics. Many books on Christ that didn't get into the Bible. Also pieces by Plato, Zoroaster, Hermes Trismegistus, Asclepius and others.

Saward, Jeff. 1987. *The Caerdroia Field Guide*. 53 Thundersley Grove, Thundersley, Benfleet, Essex, SS7 3EB, England: Caerdroia. Names and locations of mazes all over the British Isles. Excellent.

Schultz, Joachim. 1986. *Movement and Ryhthms of the Stars: A Guide to Naked-eye Observation of Sun, Moon, and Planets*. Hudson, New York: Anthroposophic Press & Floris Books, Edinburgh, Scotland. A modern view of how the ancients saw the Sun, Moon and planets.

Sjöö, Monica, & Barbara Mor. 1987. *The Great Cosmic Mother Of All: Rediscovering the Religion of the Earth*. San Francisco: Harper & Row. The entire panorama of women's herstory. An excellent work.

Spretnak, Charlene. 1984. *Lost Goddesses of Early Greece*. Boston: Beacon Press. A collection of Pre-Hellenic Myths. c.1978

Starhawk. 1982. *Dreaming the Dark*. Boston: Beacon Press. Herstory. Especially good on the witch persecutions.

Stone, Merlin. 1976. *When God Was a Woman*. New York & London: Harvest Books (Harcourt, Brace, Jovanovich). (Published in England as *The Paradise Papers*.) One of the first feminist herstorians.

Thom, A. 1974. *Megalithic Sites in Britain*. London: Oxford University Press. Sacred geometry, including the right-angled triangle, as the basis of the construction of Britain's stone rings.

von Däniken, Erich. 1972. *Chariots of the Gods?* New York: Bantam Books. First printed 1970. An early challenge to the traditional view of prehistory.

Waters, Frank. *Book of the Hopi*. New York: Penguin Books. A good overview of these fascinating Native Americans.

Watkins, Alfred. 1977. *The Old Straight Track*. London: Abacus. First published in 1925. The seminal book on leys.

MAGAZINES & PERIODICALS

Caerdroia—Edited and Published by Jeff and Deb Saward. The Caerdroia Project, 53 Thundersley Grove, Thundersley, Benfleet, Essex SS7 3EB, England. Published once yearly, certainly the best magazine in the English language dedicated entirely to labyrinths. Write to the Sawards for further information. Each issue (depending on length) will vary in price.

Clan Destiny—occasional publication of the Seneca Historical Society, 1211 Brant-Reservation Road, Brant, New York 14027-0136. Messages from Grandmother Twylah Nitsch and the Seneca Wolf Clan Lodge.

Design Spirit—A relatively new magazine dealing with sacred geometry and geomancy. Write to Design Spirit, 438 Third Street, Brooklyn, New York 11215, USA. $16.00 for four issues.

woman of power—published quarterly by woman of power, Inc., P.O. Box 827, Cambridge, Massachusetts 02238, USA. $24 for four issues, $32 foreign. A leading magazine of feminist herstory (prehistory).

ORGANIZATIONS

American Society of Dowsers. All kinds of dowsing. Conventions and gatherings all around the USA. Many local chapters. Good for books and dowsing supplies. Write ASD, P.O. Box 24, Danville, Vermont 05828 USA. phone (802) 684-3417.

Oak Dragon Camps—Outdoor nine day camps near sacred sites in England and Wales. Often has labyrinths at its camps. Write Oak Dragon Project, Box 5, Castle Cary, Somerset BA7 7YQ, England.

Sig Lonegren Apprenticeship Training Programs—Ten month, one weekend a month program in the construction and use of sacred space. Contact Sig at Box 218, Greensboro, Vermont 05841, USA. Or call (802) 533-2240 for further information.

Year of the Maze (1991)—further information can be obtained from The Maze Society, Capel Manor College, Bullsmoor Lane, Enfield, Middlesex EN1 4RQ, England. Subscriptions £10 per year.

INDEX

GOTHIC IMAGE PUBLICATIONS

Gothic Image Publications is a Glastonbury-based imprint dedicated to publishing books and pamphlets that offer a new and radical approach to our perception of the world in which we live.

As ideas about the nature of life change, we aim to make available those new perspectives which clarify our understanding of ourselves and the Earth we share.

Devas, Fairies and Angels: A Modern Approach
William Bloom

Dragons—Their History and Symbolism
Janet Hoult

Eclipse of the Sun:
An Investigation into Sun & Moon Myths
Janet McCrickard

Euphonics
John Michell

The Glastonbury Festivals
Lynne Elstob & Anne Howe

Glastonbury—Maker of Myths
Frances Howard-Gordon

The Glastonbury Tor Maze
Geoffrey Ashe

The Green Lady and the King of Shadows
A Glastonbury Legend

Hargreaves' New Illustrated Bestiary
Joyce Hargreaves

Meditation in a Changing World
William Bloom

Needles of Stone Revisited
Tom Graves

New Light on the Ancient Mystery of Glastonbury
John Michell

Spiritual Dowsing
Sig Lonegren

GOTHIC IMAGE
PUBLICATIONS

GOTHIC IMAGE PUBLICATIONS, 7 HIGH STREET, GLASTONBURY, SOMERSET BA6 9DP, ENGLAND

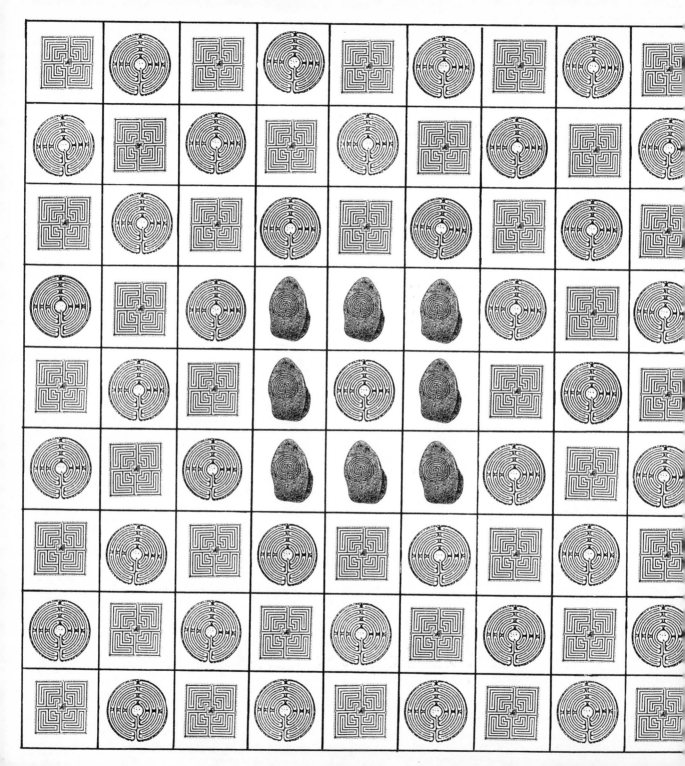